USING LETTERS IN ART AND CRAFT

USING LETTERS IN ART AND CRAFT

Carol Walklin

B T Batsford Limited London and Sydney

To my father C J J

© Carol Walklin 1974
First published 1974
ISBN 0 7134 2867 8

Filmset by Keyspools Limited
Golborne, Lancashire
Printed and bound in Great Britain by
William Clowes and Sons Limited
Beccles, Suffolk
for the publishers B T Batsford Limited
4 Fitzhardinge Street, London W1H OAH
and 23 Cross Street, Brookvale
NSW 2100, Australia

contents

acknowledgment

I acknowledge gratefully the following kind people who have helped me to prepare this book: my husband, Colin, who took the majority of the photographs and who gave support and good advice; Mary Newland for her co-operation, and for the work lent me by some of her students at Sidney Webb College of Education, London; staff and pupils at Ravensbourne School for Girls, Bromley, at Hawes Down Junior School, West Wickham, at Hayes Junior School, Bromley, at Blackheath High Junior School, and at the Print Department at Forest Hill School for Boys; Anne Stone of the Art Department, Stockwell College of Education, Bromley; Eirian Short for designing the quilted letter; and all those who loaned me books and photographs.

I should like to thank all the helpful people at the Library and Circulation Department of the Victoria and Albert Museum, and Thelma M Nye for her guidance.

I thank my family too, for their forbearance, and Ella Brown who, as always, coped when I could not.

C W   1974

introduction

The letter, in its many aspects, is an area of study both rich and fascinating. It can intrigue and challenge every kind of intellect as well as provide a useful and often simple springboard for good design.

The illustrations in this book are taken mainly from actual classroom projects involving age groups ranging from the infant school to colleges of further education. Many of these projects are adaptable and can be altered to suit individual requirements and limitations.

Expertise in the actual creation of letterforms is not emphasized in this book. The letters here are being used as a means to convey emotions, pass on information, stimulate an interest in harmony, colour or tone. In fact, there are very few teaching points in the art and design field that cannot be complemented by the study and intelligent use of the letter and its antecedents. A large number of the activities described here have not begun as specific art lessons *per se*, but have arisen out of general topics connected with other subjects, particularly the work done with younger children.

If high standards of design are to be achieved, we need a public who will recognize the good from the bad, the tasteful from the tasteless, and demand not only integrity but good presentation. It is therefore the part of the art educationalist to combat much of the mass media which almost indoctrinates the young with its bombardment of the senses. Many of the exercises here are intended to do this by increasing visual awareness and heightening discrimination.

I

Some of the illustrations are from work by established artists and designers. The purpose of all the pictures, however (which range from the first wobbly efforts of the infant writer to the confident designs of the professional) is to demonstrate that the letter has served Man well and can continue to do so by communicating, stimulating, decorating and identifying.

Using the letter in art education can help develop techniques that will give both satisfaction and pleasure.

2 Lettering on a fairground trailer. Photograph by Herbert Spencer RDI Dr RCA FSIAD

1 signs and symbols

Twentieth century technology has outpaced the traveller's command of language. The fields of science, commerce and transport have created a situation where the need for quick, unmistakable communication has stimulated a revival of the universal language of signs and symbols.

3 Symbols for the 1964 Olympic Games at Tokyo, designed under the direction of Masaru Katzumie

4 Northwest American family totems
above Raven
below Beaver

5 *right* Prehistoric African cave painting

Historical background

To appreciate fully present-day symbology it is useful to look back to a time when signs and symbols were the main means of communication, in the days before the alphabet.

Prehistoric and primitive cave paintings appear to provide information as well as aesthetic satisfaction. Looking at examples of these in the classroom can promote discussion as to their true purpose. Often situated in a dark and remote corner of the cave, apart from the main dwelling areas, it is questionable whether they are merely for decoration. They may record past successes, hope for the future; but whether factual communications or invocations, many of them are creations of lasting magic and beauty.

There have been, and still are, substitutes for the written letter: notched sticks, wampum belts, Braille, Morse, semaphore. Less prosaic than these are the carvings of the American Indian and the Eskimo, where there is often a happy combination of an accurate record or chain of thought with sensitive and decorative craftsmanship.

While discussing with the children or students the antecedents of the letter, it is interesting to trace the development of our present Western alphabet through the pictogram, ideogram and hieroglyph to the all-important step: the use of phonetics.

Ideograms were a development of the pictogram. Where previously the drawing of a foot would simply represent a foot, now it could have a wider implication with a more abstract interpretation, such as distance, walking or running.

6 Detail from a Western Eskimo engraved walrus tusk. Reproduced by courtesy of the Trustees of the British Museum

7 *right* Mayan altar tablet

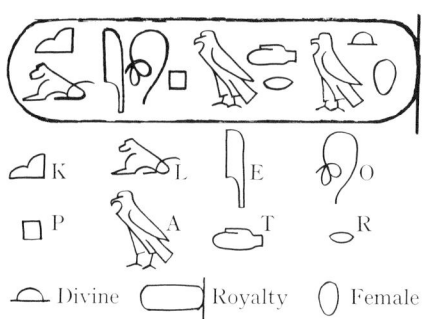

△◁ K   L   E   O

□ P   A   T   R

⌒ Divine   ▢ Royalty   ◯ Female

8 Kleopatra. Diagram of Egyptian cartouche at Philae. Three of the signs represent whole words, the other symbols represent individual letters. This tendency to mix pictograms, ideograms and phonograms has made deciphering difficult. Taken from an illustration in Jackdaw No. 47 *The Development of Writing* by courtesy of the publishers

9 Chinese calligraphy, tenth century AD, meaning 'thunder and lightning'

Various civilizations such as the Sumerian, Chinese, Aztec and Mayan have used pictures to represent whole words.

Progressing towards syllabic or phonetic writing, the Egyptian hieroglyph can be discussed. The study of this system shows the use of a combination of signs that represent both words and individual letters.

These hieroglyphs provided information but were used in such a way that whether on papyrus, linen, metal or stone, they were at the same time both functional and elegant.

At the point where phonetic writing develops, it is of interest to note the division which comes culturally as well as visually between the Asiatic brush forms and the early alphabets leading to the invention of movable type.

10 *Group W* by Paul Klee. Copyright by S.P.A.D.E.M., Paris, 1973

2 the symbol and letter as design units

Before starting to make use of letterless symbols and actual letters, it stimulates some serious thought to consider what life would be like without this set of universally accepted symbols.

Thought can be 'preserved in a permanent present, a pure world of mind and thought stored in the sensuous material of paper and ink. If we think of what a university, say, would be without a single book, and without blackboards and notebooks, shut off from a vanished and irrecoverable past, we should have a picture of the limitations which *time* sets upon oral speech alone, as an instrument of conscious mind'. (Professor R. A. Wilson in *The Miraculous Birth of Language*, J. M. Dent and Sons.)

11 Shields from *Des Armes des Chevaliers de la Table Ronde*, a sixteenth-century book of coloured Coats of Arms. Reproduced by courtesy of the Victoria and Albert Museum

Heraldic symbols

Having considered the state of a world that has never had the alphabet, the discussion can be continued with an introduction to the symbols that have been used in heraldry. Here the medieval designer and craftsman has had to provide communications that were recognisable immediately and with no chance of error. It would be a matter of no little importance that on the battlefield each person should be able to distinguish friend from foe. In more peaceful times it would be necessary to establish ownership as well as allegiance: to know who owned the land, served which master or mistress.

The rebus

In addition to the many divisions and colourings of badges, banners, Coats of Arms, there existed a variation called a rebus. This was a pictorial representation of a name or object, using the syllables or parts of the word, interpreted in a literal form, a kind of visual pun.

Making a rebus can be a good exercise in economical and decorative designing. It requires ingenuity to produce a design that covers the word and is also pleasing to look at. See figure 12.

Subjects for the rebus can be the names of towns and counties, people or the school. Clubs and teams are popular subjects, and badges or soccer-ground flags can provide an exercise in problem-solving with a strong personal interest.

The finished designs can be carried out in black ink and pen. This restriction of using black only encourages the best use of solid areas combined with textured, decorative areas.

It is helpful to show examples of drawings by Bewick, Beardsley and Ravilions, and to collect pictures from magazines (*The Radio Times* is a good source), in order to discuss techniques and merit. It should be emphasized how valuable are the 'whites'. Using black paper and white paint can assist this appreciation, particularly for those with a tentative approach with the pen.

Colour can be introduced (the Coats of Arms illustrated left are hand tinted) and according to age and interest, research can be made into the terms and divisions of heraldry.

12 *above and overleaf* Rebuses by fourteen and fifteen year old children
a Elephant and Castle

A variation of this project could be to translate the two-dimensional work into three-dimensional, carrying it out in clay or *Plasticine*. For this a tile could be made with a bas-relief design, or alternatively, the design could be depressed to make a mould from which casts could be taken.

Hobo signs and runes

Another form of picture-writing, with the look of a letter, is the hobo sign made by tramps. These signs communicate, pass on

12b *above* Robinson
12c *below* Tunbridge Wells

information, bridging the gap made by illiteracy. They are not so secretive as Masonic signs and they lack some of the beauty of runic devices.

Runes (the letters of the earliest Teutonic alphabet, or a similar mark of mysterious significance) were sometimes used to produce positive results, but in the main were decorative memorials or magical spells. Their meaning is often not understood, but the lines and spaces formed on the areas that they cover are usually satisfying in their balance and arrangement.

The frequent use of wood as a base is the explanation for the characteristic shape of the rune. It was difficult to make horizontal strokes with a knife following the grain of the wood, and to avoid this, all the strokes were vertical or slanting.

In *The Hobbit* by Tolkien, runes were inscribed round the door as protection.

Young children enjoy inventing spells and could be asked to make their own magical devices. Older children can try to form a combination of hobo-like signs that will convey a message without using any actual letterforms – a symbolic sentence.

13 Swedish runic stones from Uppland

14 Hobo signs
a   out
b   camp here
c   dog
d   sick
e   nothing

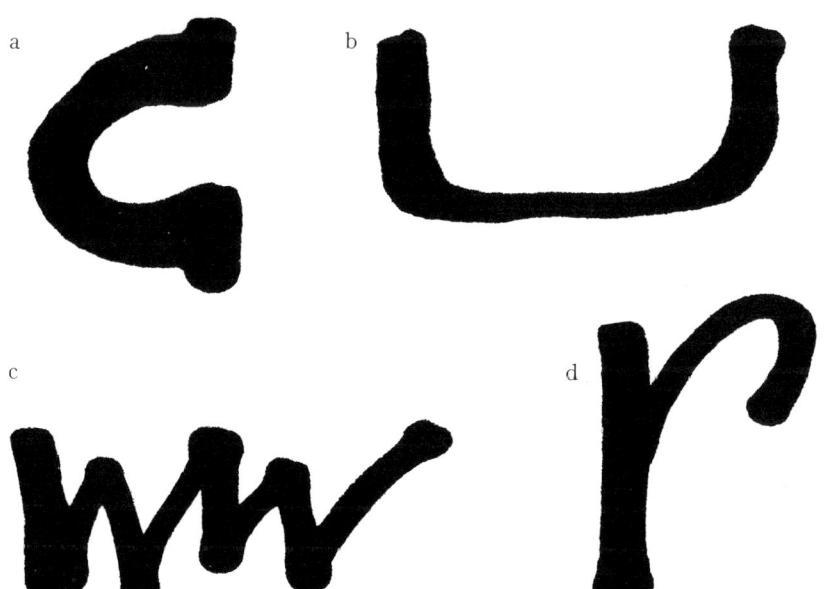

3 marks and monograms

Trademarks

Symbolic design also appears in the form of trademarks. A discussion point can be why there are nearly twice as many trade*marks* as trade-*names*. Is it because diagrams and graphic representations convey information more rapidly, efficiently and universally than verbal descriptions?

15   Trademarks and symbols
a   *top*   Trademark of Volkswagen Limited
b   *above*   Trademark of Armitage Shanks Limited
c   *right*   Registered trademark for the British Steel Corporation, designed by David Gentleman

The necessity for economy and simplicity in the creation of a trademark makes it an exercise which, like the rebus, requires for its solution ingenuity in addition to a conscious effort to create pleasing spaces and shapes. Unlike the rebus, however, letterforms are often interwoven with pictorial symbols to form the design, and some have actual letters subtly changed into significant shapes. (See *Working Words*, page 86.)

The mark itself can be described as a kind of signature. It identifies the owner, manufacturer or sponsor and shows his pride or responsibility in his produce or service. It is used for quick and accurate identification of tiny objects, such as pills, or for identifying vast industrial combines.

Collecting examples of trademarks, those with letterforms and those without, will create an interest in the subject. Criticisms

16 *below and overleaf* A student teacher's exploitation of a trade symbol, based on the letter A

a Scored paper sculpture

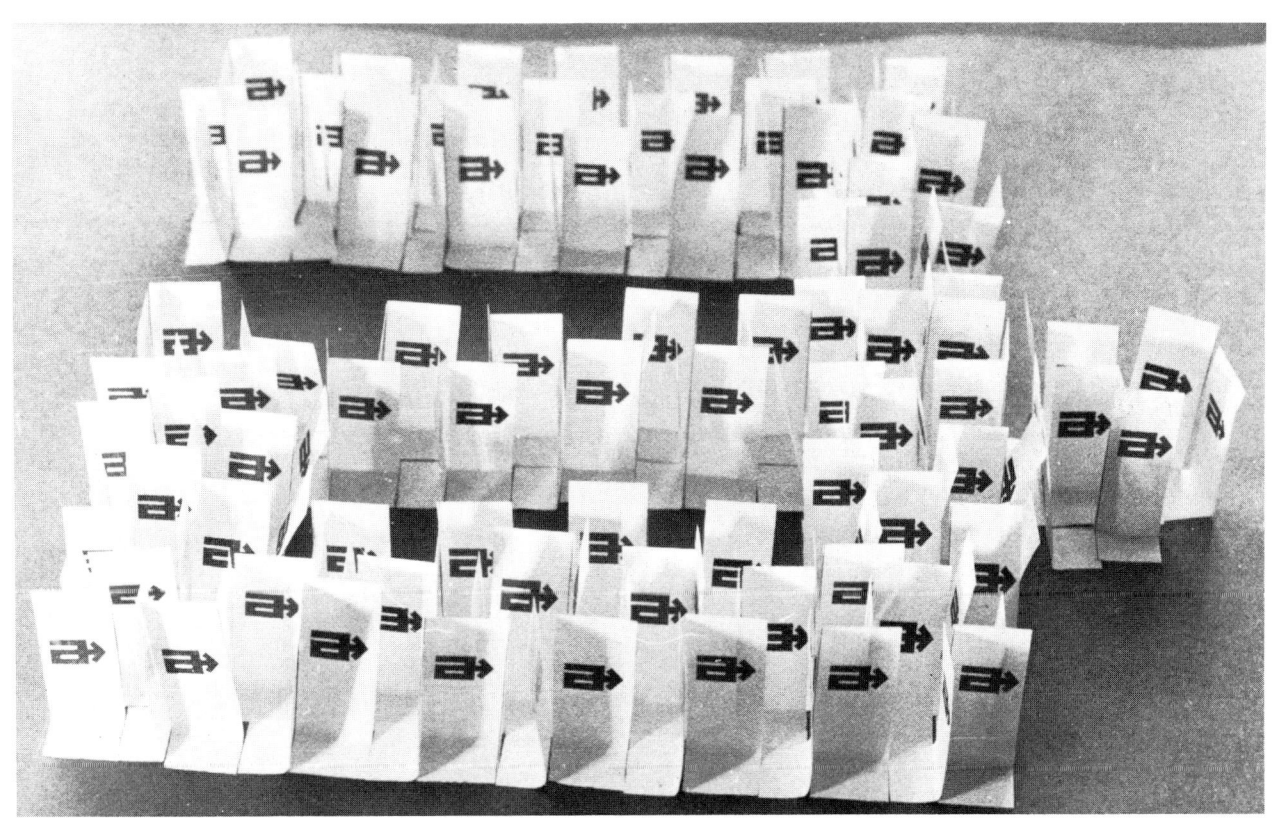

should be invited and possible alternatives. It should be pointed out, though, that there are three main criteria for a good trademark and that it is not an easy job to include them all unless one has considerable expertise and experience. These criteria are:

1 That the trademark can be reduced in size if necessary, but still maintain its legibility – this affects the spacing of the shapes.

2 It must be unique and memorable.

3 It must be adaptable to interpretations in various media and techniques of reproduction.

It is a highly sophisticated problem and the younger age groups should not be asked to design a trademark but rather to appraise existing ones, so that by observation and discussion their ability for discrimination will be increased.

16b   Nails positioned in softwood

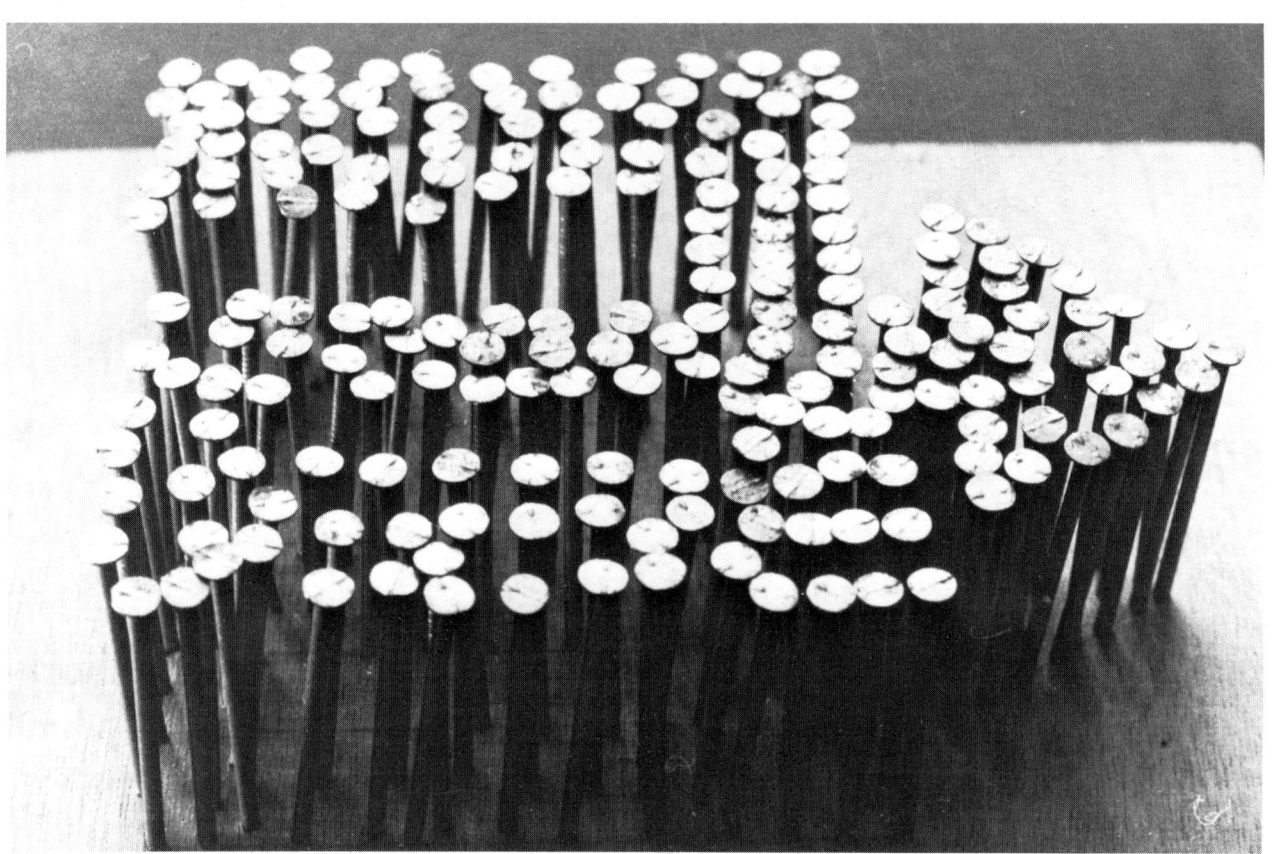

17 Panel by Mary Kirwan, showing a brand name used as part of a design. Emerald green silk embroidered in scarlet and orange-red wools and stranded cotton

Monograms

Simplicity and elegance are characteristics to be found in many of the monograms of the Greek, Roman and Byzantine cultures, also in the early Christian symbols. Here the actual letters are often hard to distinguish as they have been arranged back to front, upside-down, or are only partially shown. This concealment serves to make them intriguing as well as decorative.

Many of the early astronomical signs, printer's and mason's marks, watermarks on hand-made and bond papers, have pleasing combinations and balance. In more recent times functional and decorative designs have been produced, in Spain and America particularly, as cattle brands to identify the ranches and owners.

18 *top* Friedrick I (Barbarossa), Holy Roman Emperor, 1123–1190
19 *centre* Monogram from *The Book of Signs* by Rudolph Koch
20 *below* Watermark. France, 1593

21 *top* Printer's mark. Octavianus Scotus, Venice, 1493
22 *below* Merchant's mark

23 *top* Engraver's mark. Germany, late sixteenth century
24 Cattle brands
a *centre* Dona Juana de Figueroa, Ecuador, 1593
b *below* Bob on the Square Ranch, Texas, 1870

4 initial and individual letters

Although there are ever-changing fashions in the methods of teaching children to read, eventually the would-be reader must memorise each individual letter that is part of the accepted alphabet.

An exercise which may help the younger age groups to reinforce their learning, and, at the same time, form part of their art education, is the 'spreading initial'.

Each child selects one letter which is then drawn in the centre of the paper. See figures 25 and 26. The letter could be printed by the child, or alternatively, cut out of a magazine. It is then surrounded with drawings of objects that begin with this initial letter. These first drawings should touch the letter at one point, then each new picture touch its neighbour and so on until the letter is the centre of a radiating collection of objects. Older children should be encouraged to keep looking at the effect they are creating and to use the areas with thought, so that the work becomes decorative as well as inventive. The young ones may need some assistance with choosing the objects, depending on their ability, and group work with plenty of drawing space may sometimes be preferable.

25　*top*　Central letter with spreading pictures drawn by a twelve year old child
26　*above*　Central letter with spreading pictures drawn by a fifteen year old child

The isolated letter is in its own right a significant symbol, but there is a positive preoccupation with the initial as part of one's *own* identity, resulting in the scarring of many a tree-trunk and desk-lid. Whether it is a sultan's grandiose flourish, or a humbler finger-print, this kind of mark is unique and personal. It is also very powerful as it can legalize, acknowledge and approve.

27 Seal and signature of Abdul-Medjid Ibn Mahmud, a Turkish sultan, 1822–1861 (enlarged)
28 Fingerprint

عبد المجيد خان ابن محمود المظفر دائما

This uniqueness is apparent in the personal plaques produced by eight and nine year old and twelve year old children. See figures 29 and 10. As a design exercise it teaches ways of dividing a given area, visual communication and can promote further learning from historical sources.

The plaques made by the younger children developed from discussions on medieval battles and the need for heraldry, birthday signs, and their own initials. Using some or all of these units, the children then designed a personal 'badge'. These were presented as paper blocks based on a circle of common diameter so that, when all were completed, they could be made into a long frieze of rubbings (frottage).

Some of the plaques made by the twelve year olds were sprayed with aerosol paint on completion. These profited by having a fairly high relief. Others were used as printing blocks, and in this case the children had to consider if any of their units would lose their significance if they appeared back to front when printed. If so, they had to employ *reversal* of the block.

29 Rubbings of plaques made by eight and nine year old children
a *left* EP (birthday sign Pisces and likes swimming)
b *right* RA (Crystal Palace supporter and gardener)

The art of masking a print can be taught with the printing process. Sometimes the design will benefit by a textured background, at other times a really clean edge is preferable. This is obtained by using a mask. A mask can be made from a rubbing or a dry light print (a duplicate of the print to be masked). Cut away the actual image, plus a surround of about 2 mm (1/10 in.), which will help with the positioning. The printed piece is discarded, and the *surround* kept. (Usually you are presented with the image and the surround goes in the waste-bin if you are not explicit.)

30 Birthday sign plaques by fourteen and fifteen year old children
a *left* LR (Cancer) b *below left* Susan (Leo) (masked)
c *below right* Susan (Leo) (unmasked)

Examples of initials from past centuries make fascinating study. These decorated letters are descended from two different traditions, one combining abstract tracery and geometric patterns, and the other zoomorphic letters, composed almost entirely of birds and fishes: on one side the use of the ruler and the compass, and on the other, brush-drawn, richly decorative flora and fauna.

31   Quilted C by Eirian Short reminiscent of medieval initials. The corded quilting was done by hand in back stitch

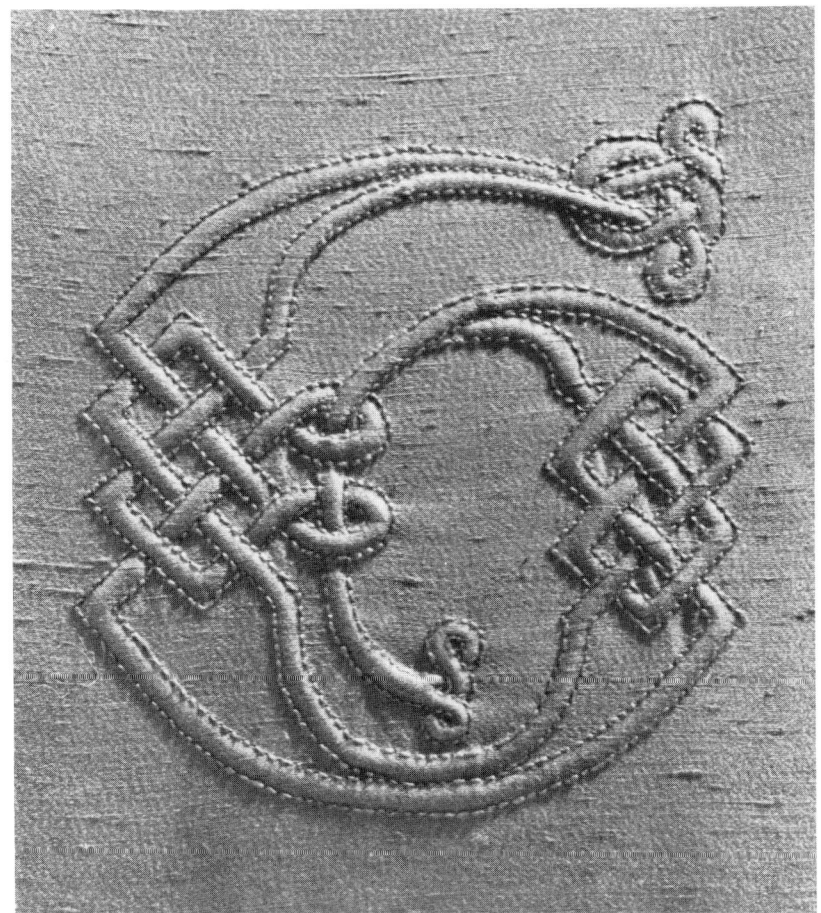

32a   *top*   Initial Λ (showing the Virgin Walpurga) from a twelfth-century German manuscript in the Württembergische Landesbibliothek, Stuttgart
32b   *above*   Initial T (showing the Holy the Holy Martyrs Prunus and Felicianus) from a twelfth-century manuscript in the Württembergische Landesbibliothek, Stuttgart

33 Two Hs
a *above* Decorative letter in wax
crayon by a nine year old boy
b *right* Serpent H from a manuscript
writing book copied from an alphabet
engraved by the Master of the
Banderolles. England, *circa* 1550.
Reproduced by courtesy of the Victoria
and Albert Museum

It is unlikely that anyone in the classroom, however, will have
a suitably monastic and peacefully orientated atmosphere in
which to imitate these wonderful designs. The anecdotal details
and satisfying patterns are, nevertheless, worth studying, and a
modern version could be made, recounting some incident, real or
imaginary (figure 34); celebrating an event; or making a birthday
sign like the B and Cancer design (figure 35).

The following illustrations show different types of work by children and students, using individual letters.

34 *left* Initial O with Saint George and the Dragon, based on a medieval manuscript. Single block linocut, printed in six colours by a fifteen year old girl
35 *below* Initial B with Cancer sign by a student

36 *opposite* Picture of a bill poster
with letter A by an eight year old boy,
using cut paper, crayon and paint
37 *above* BHS. Initials of the school
used to form linear patterns to fill a
rectangle by a nine year old girl

38　Two arrangements of cut paper
letterforms to illustrate interlocking and
overlapping by a student

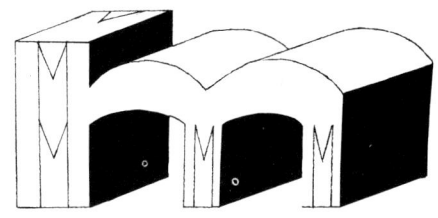

39 *above left* Tonal exercise in red fabrics by a twelve year old girl
40 *above* An exercise in pen and ink to create a three-dimensional effect with one letter, by a fourteen year old girl
41 *left* Fabric design. Woodblock A printed over a striped fabric by a student

5 names

The single letter has been proved useful as an extension of the learning and experimenting process and in showing the importance of space and pattern in general designing.

The whole name can also be put to good use. Again, with the younger groups in nursery school, emphasis is given to the naming of objects and to the child's own, personal 'label'. Just to paint his name, freely, with no restriction as to scale or numbers of colours, can produce spontaneous results which give obvious satisfaction to the young painter. When a little more control has been developed, the child can paint his name along the horizontal

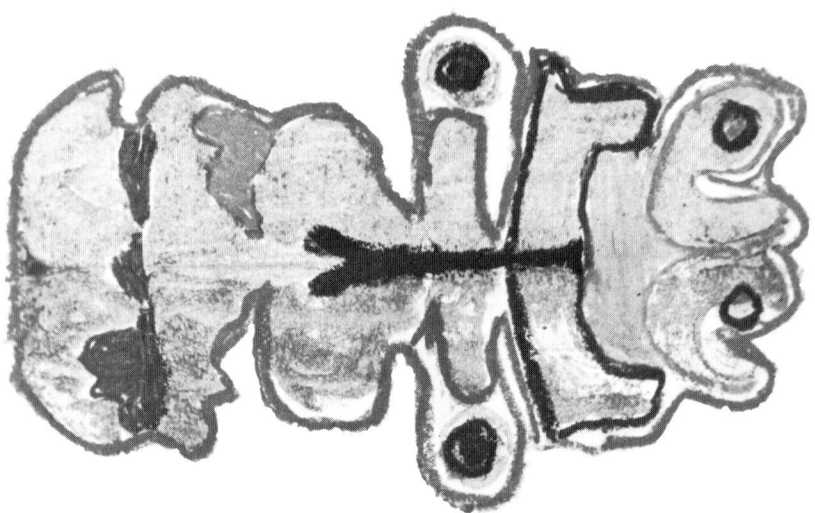

42 Name blot by a six year old child

fold of a piece of paper, then refold the paper and 'blot' the name, achieving a mirror-image. This shape can be left as it is, or developed by echoing the rhythms of the name in line or colour (figure 42). According to Lewis Carroll's Humpty Dumpty, a name *must* have a meaning: '*My* name means the shape that I am – and a good handsome shape it is too.' These painted names will hardly be the child's shape, but new shapes will be made by each individual and every mark will be unique. The despairing cry of 'But I can't *draw*' can always be answered with the statement that if you can write your name, or indeed make any mark, this is, albeit very basic, a sort of drawing. Any experimenting with colour and pattern will help to build up confidence in the handling of various materials. Simple tasks such as these that involve a comfortably familiar thing, one's own name or initials, will enable the child to approach successive tasks in the field of art and design with greater self assurance.

A name unit is also featured in the mug design. This project, illustrated here in two forms, helps to underline the fact that a design made for one material is not necessarily suitable for

43 Preparatory work for a mug design. Coloured panel made with felt tip pen by a fourteen year old boy

44 Paper blocks by fourteen year old
girls
a Anne
b Lizzy

exploitation in another, at least not without a certain amount of adaptation. In other words, one must always design for the limitations of the chosen media. One version here is carried out in cartridge paper or thin card, the other in ceramics. The precise shapes created with paper and scissors were characteristic of the technique of the first version, but when the same pupils were given the opportunity for making a pottery mug, they discovered for themselves that most of the designs were unsuitable for the more fluid medium of trailer and slip, and also the difficulties of working on a curved, hard, surface. Students who, from the start, designed decoration for this medium were more immediately successful.

The unit was to be formed from the name, nickname, birth sign, or a combination of the three. If letterforms were used, then interesting shapes were achieved by juxtaposing these, similar to the monograms (examples of which are useful to study at the outset).

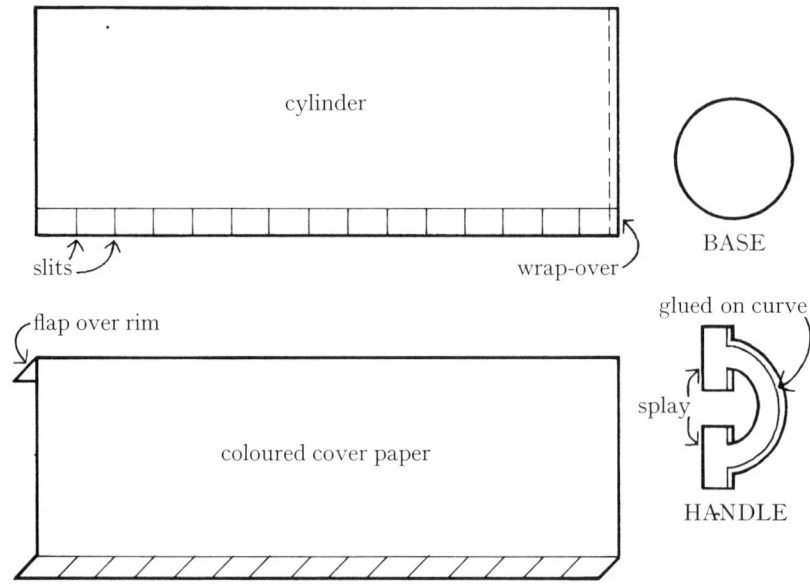

45 How to make a mug

Focusing on the spaces in between is something that has to be taught, and practice in this is invaluable, particularly if the pupils wish to study graphics at greater depth later on. The unit can be single or repeated and it should wrap around a cylinder of thin card or cartridge paper approximately 255 mm × 125 mm (10 in. × 5 in.). See figure 45.

At this stage, the unit is cut out and pasted down on a piece of firm backing paper considerably larger than the all-over size of the cylinder. This is kept, as it can be used for other subsequent design ideas (see page 39). Using this block to make rubbings, experiments should be made with the arrangements, and also the possibilities of colour ranges and counter-change. These rubbings can be wrapped around the cylinder and viewed in the round.

The space for the handle can be allowed for when positioning the design, or a natural space may fall without disturbing the balance. The character of the handle should match the unit.

46 Paper mugs with names and birthday signs by fourteen year old girls

47 *above* Paper mug with the name
Kathy
48 *right* Slip-cast mug and bowl made
in a one-piece mould. The handle was
made separately

49 *opposite* Debbie. Preparatory work
for a thematic collage by a fourteen year
old girl
a *top right* Block
b *centre right* Rubbing
c *below left* Scaled-up drawing for
collage
d *below right* Collage on the theme of
hair. Photographs of fur, wool and hair,
and real wool and silk threads were used

Original methods of fixing and shaping the handle should be
encouraged, bearing in mind that this is an imitation of a *functional* object and that therefore the handle should be practical as
well as pleasing visually.

A useful exercise is one which can teach a simple method of
enlarging or reducing a piece of work, in proportion. See figure 49.

A clear rubbing of the unit is taken and contained in a rectangle.
It is made in the lower left-hand corner of the paper. A diagonal is
drawn from the lower left-hand corner of the rubbing and taken
up and beyond the unit, right to the edge of the paper. Extend the
base line until it is the required width of the new, bigger size.
Continue the line vertically until it reaches the diagonal, then
left, horizontally, until it reaches an extension of the left vertical
container line. This new rectangle is now in proportion to the
original one. To match the unit, bisect or square up the small
version; trace off the new size onto some backing board or paper,
and draw an identical grid. Note where various points fall and
mark these in on the enlargement. To reduce a large picture,
simply reverse the procedure, still using the diagonal. This is a
useful method, particularly where pupils are designing units such
as trademarks where it is necessary to show alternative sizings.

The enlarged design unit can form the basis for a thematic collage. The ready-made areas which make up the unit enable the pupil to give all his attention to the interpretation of the theme and to the technique of collage. The subject matter can be straightforward colour schemes or colour ranges, or textures, using wallpaper sample books which give a good variety (but it is best if only *one* colour is chosen). Older students can devise their own themes such as music, air, the festive season, features.

The materials for the panels can be fabric and thread, pasta and string, beads and buttons, magazine and painted pictures, or any combination of these that helps to create the right feeling. It is beneficial to decide on the type of collage material and then use an appropriate backing, as if the children envisage a collection of nuts and bolts, or pebbles, obviously it is imperative to have a really tough background. Carton sides are suitable for heavier work, and either wallpaper paste or resin glue may be used for the adhesive.

A simpler version for the younger child could involve one big letter, not too slender in shape. This would be drawn so that it touches the edges of the paper. Alternatively, a combination of two letters could be arranged, but in both instances the shapes they make in the rectangle should be considered carefully. The interspaces and counterspaces are then coloured in with crayon.

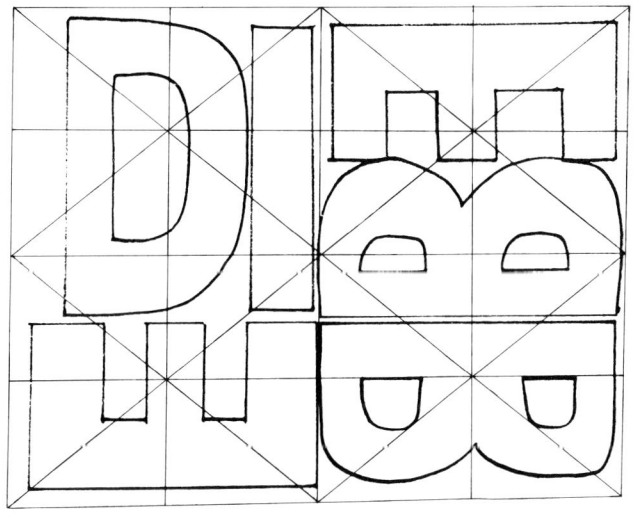

This is preferable to paint, as sometimes the glue picks up the colour which spoils the thread or fabric that is being stuck down. Some of the coloured areas are then filled in with spiralled threads that follow the shapes, emphasising them; or small snipped pieces of fabric or paper are used to fill in the larger, simpler areas. This type of work helps the children's manual dexterity as well as reinforcing their experience of colour, particularly if they try to match the thread or fabric colour to that which appears initially in crayon.

Names can be used for fabric printing. See figure 50. The fabric in figure 51 has been printed with a flocked lino-block. The design is based on the name 'Susan'. Various ways of using the block were tried and the one illustrated shows a rotation of the block printed in one colour.

50 Preparation for fabric printing by fourteen year old girls. Linoprints, using paint on newsprint
a Sue
b *opposite* Lou

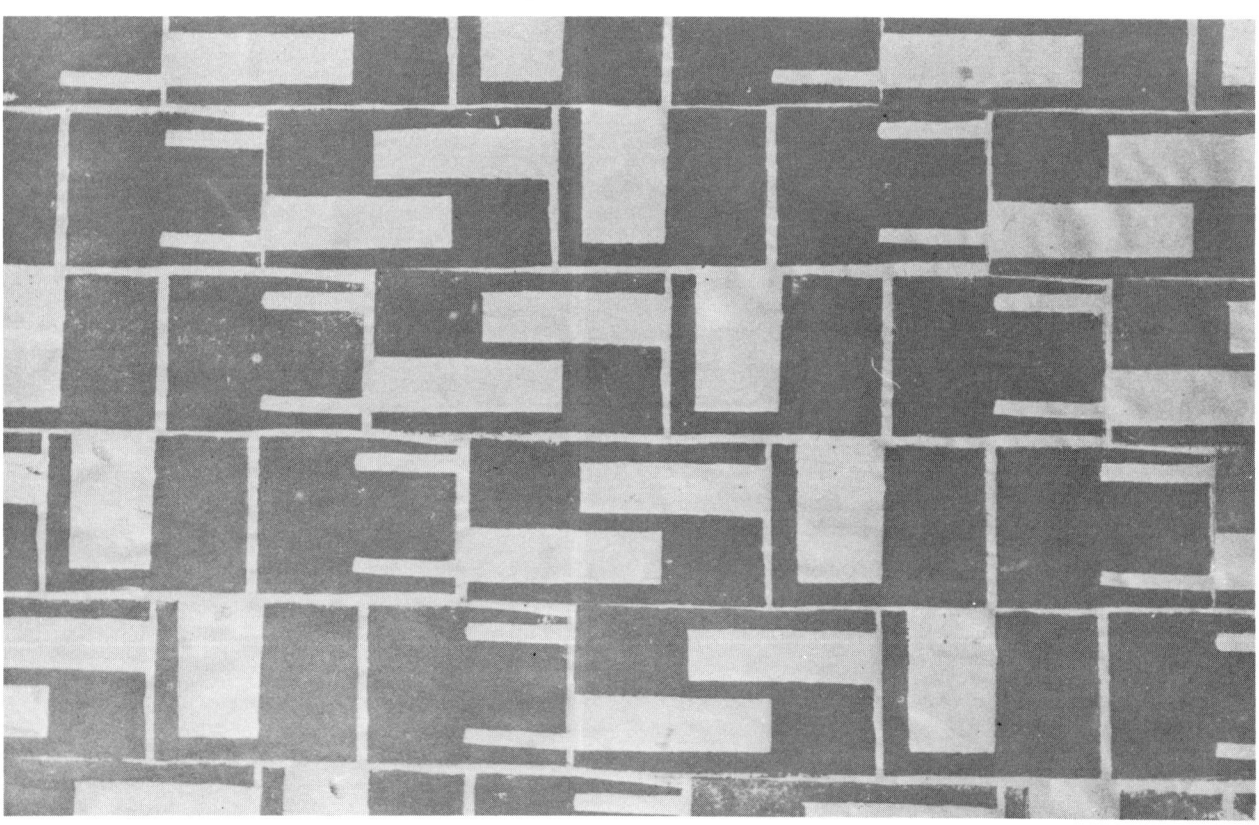

51 Susan. Fabric print in black on
white by a student. Linoblock, flocked
and mounted on wood

6 alphabets: faces and families

The main influences in the actual formation of letterforms can be said to be tools, speed and space. Awareness of these factors can be stimulated by experiment. Cuneiform writing, Roman chiselled letters, medieval manuscript writing and runic inscriptions all illustrate these points.

52 G drawn with different tools

Gay dainty flowers go swiftly to decay, poor wretched life's short portion flies away, we eat, we drink, we sleep; but lo, anon, old age steals on us, never thought upon.

Mary Wakeling Ended This December The Tenth 1742 Aged Ten Years

44

53 *opposite* Sampler by Mary Wakeling, eighteenth century. Reproduced by courtesy of the Victoria and Albert Museum

54 *above* *The Barking Dog* by Shiko Munakata, 1959. Woodcut, printed in black, 18 in. × 15 in. Collection, The Museum of Modern Art, New York. Blanchette Rockefeller Fund. With slashing woodcut technique this Japanese printmaker creates a vivid white pattern on a black background

Faces

All reference books, magazines, novels, advertisements, film credits and television advertising employ a massive variety of type 'faces' (the term for various styles of letter design). Some are traditional or based on ancient styles, others are specifically made for a certain subject or situation.

The study of these variations increases visual awareness and adds to the young designer's vocabulary. Instant adhesive lettering is much in use these days, and is now allowed in certain GCE syllabuses. It is therefore very necessary to train the eye and hand to make good use of this aid. It is time-saving and can look professional when done well, but it does require careful selection and accuracy in positioning. A study of the varieties and character of letterforms will help the student to appreciate the difficulties and assets of this aid.

In Ben Shahn's *Love and Joy about Letters* (Cory Adams and MacKay) he advises us to look past the letters at the spaces *around* them. 'Letters are quantities and *spaces* are quantities and only the eye and the hand can measure them'. Anyone who has hand set type will recognise the truth of this. He also has strong words to express his feelings regarding the violations of the 'rules' – something that occurs all too often today. The insensitive mixing of thicks and thins, serifs and sans serifs he finds 'cacophonous and utterly unacceptable'.

The following exercises are designed to help the awareness of the differences that exist in letterforms and to develop the critical faculty.

1 Choose any two letters of the alphabet, then from printed matter, cut out a collection of ten different versions of each of them. Lay them out, compare them and discuss their basic differences: serifs, sans serifs, ornamented, shadow, reverse and so on. Groups can work on one letter and form a whole sheet of examples, seeing how many variations can be found at one time. Alternatively, similar styles can be collected and labelled.

2 One big initial letter is made from a collection of smaller letters, so that a large letter 'A' is composed of any variety of 'A's, including upper and lower case. If the supply is short then other letters can be added. See figure 55.

55 Two As. Paper collage letters

3   An alternative, more pictorial approach is to choose an object that has a simple shape and create a symbol made of its own initial letter. The drawing is lightly sketched in on a piece of paper about 200 mm × 150 mm (8 in. × 6 in.) and filled in with the cut-out letters. See figure 56.

56   *above and overleaf* Collages in black and white using the initial letter of the object portrayed by fourteen and fifteen year old girls
a   Bee

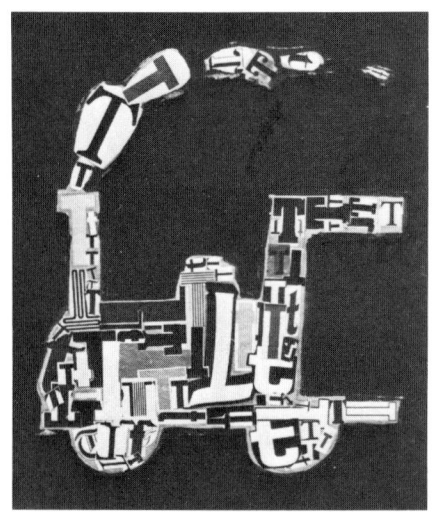

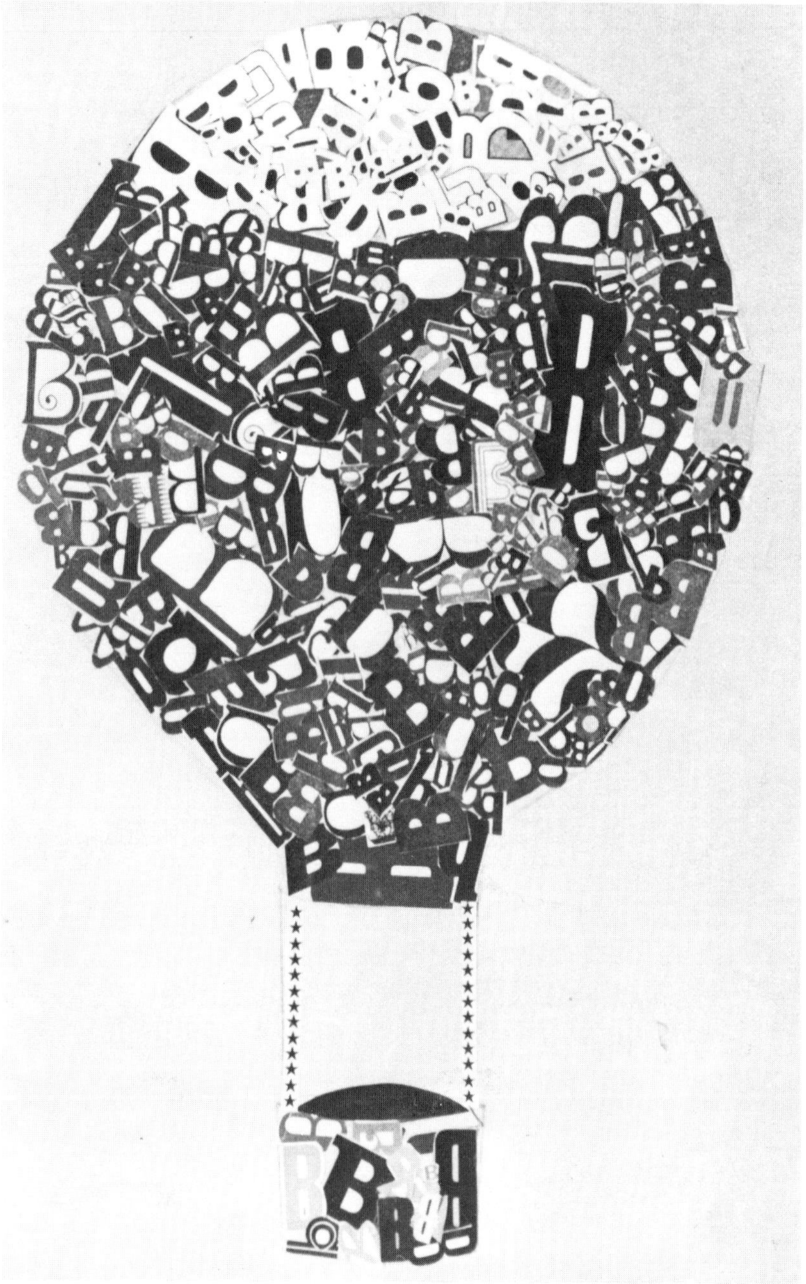

56b *top* Train
56c *above* Duck
56d *right* Balloon. The basket is made
of coloured letters

4 Another exercise to heighten the awareness of the need for legibility and the significant parts of individual letters, is to take a well-known heading or brand-name and alter it, testing for the limits of legibility. In this way it can be seen which parts of the letterform are the essential ones. See figure 57.

57 An exercise in altering and deforming a well-known heading to find the limits of legibility

5   Distortions of the individual letter: this helps to show how far the letter can be ill-treated before losing a shape. Draw a horizontal line and along this, starting with a normal letter-shape, make a series of drawings, expanding, bending, compressing and so on, until the original letter loses its identity. Different tools can be used to create varying thicknesses and quality of line. See figure 58.

Families

One of these variations (not too exotic), is taken as a typical letter of an alphabet and after some discussion of the basic 'rules' of relationships of one letter to another, an attempt is made to create a whole alphabet. See figures 59 and 60. I say an 'attempt'

58   Distortion of single letters

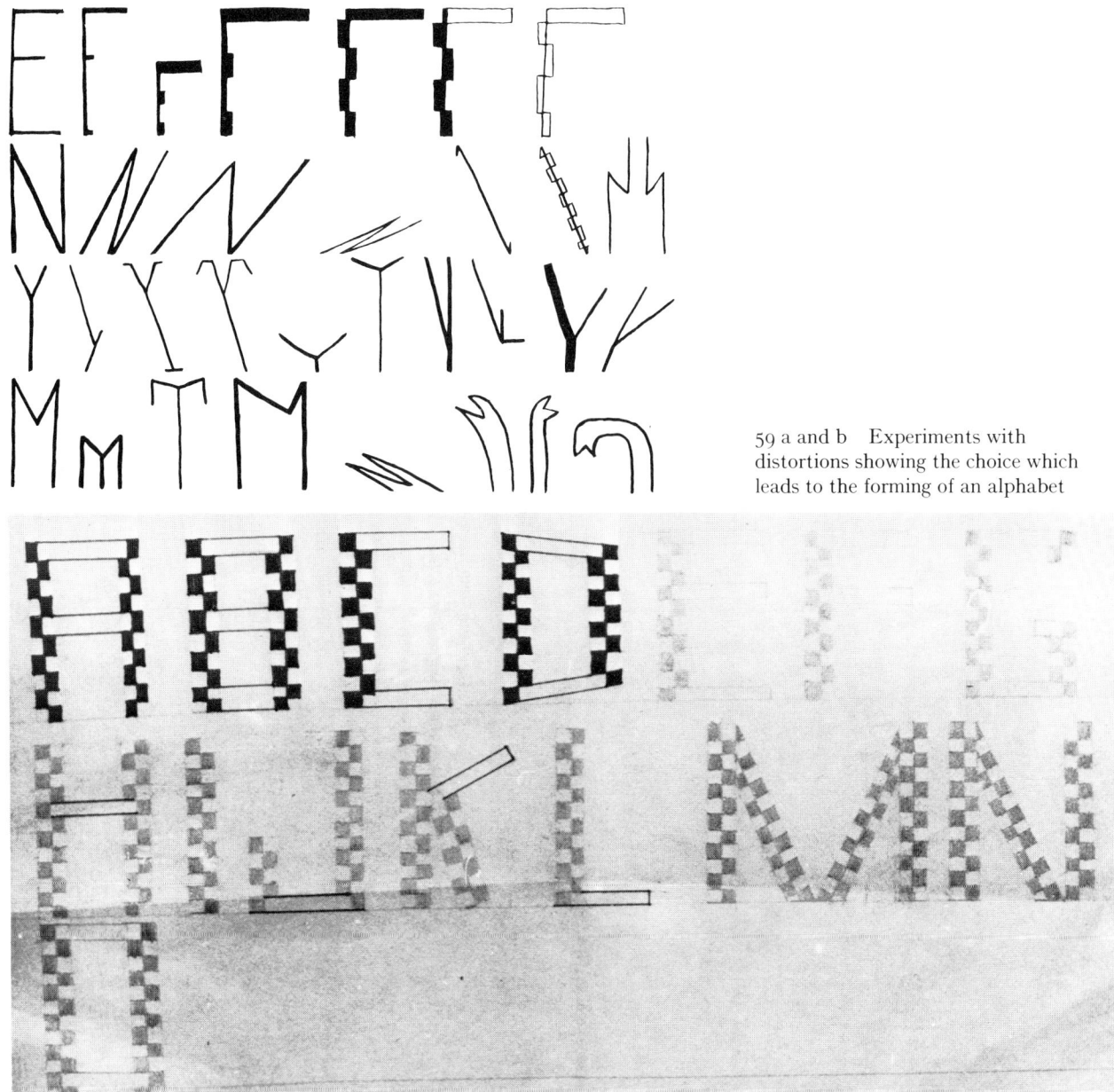

59 a and b   Experiments with distortions showing the choice which leads to the forming of an alphabet

because this task is an extremely sophisticated one, with some letters posing very real design problems. Pat Russell in her book, *Lettering for Embroidery* (Batsford) provides a very clear series of charts of rules and relationships.

The classic rules and proportions can be appreciated if not emulated. The contemporary attitude to letterforms is a very elastic one. A conventionally wide letter may stand narrowly beside its expanded, usually slimmer neighbour. Like the fluctuating hemline or waist level, so the alphabet must suffer and obey the whims of fashion. This makes it even more important that there should be some education in discrimination in matters of this kind, so that there is no easy acceptance of any solution to visual communication, albeit from a Jumble Sale poster to a popular television series. However 'odd' the alphabet there is no excuse for badly formed, badly spaced lettering.

A pictorial, or personalised alphabet is not quite such a sophisticated problem. It can be light-hearted or serious in theme, chosen by the individual or given as a set task. There are many books available providing historic examples of this kind of alphabet (see bibliography).

Nine letters or numerals were designed on one theme and then one letter chosen which was enlarged to about 160 mm × 125 mm

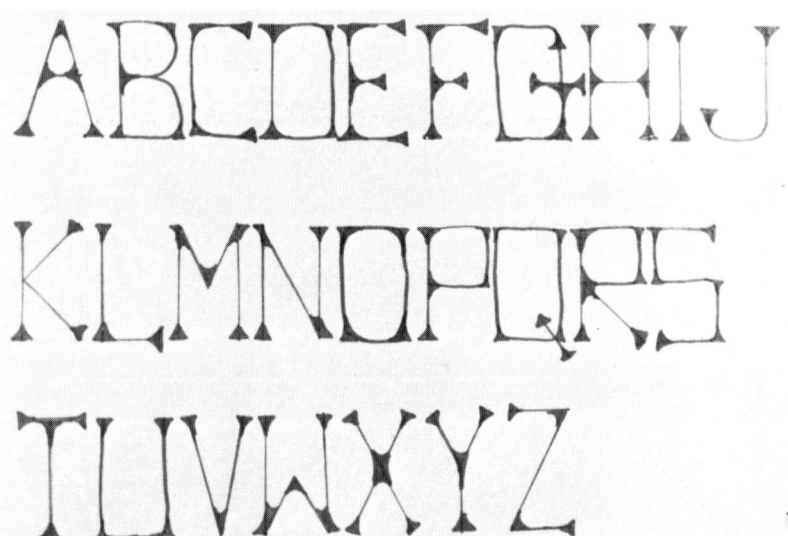

60   An alphabet by a fifteen year old girl

($6\frac{1}{2}$ in. × 5 in.) and carried out in white paint on black paper. See figure 62. In the pen and ink smaller version, a good use of a combination of lines and solids was encouraged and the satisfactory adaptation of black to white reversal.

61 *right* Mnemontechnic alphabet by Trithemius in *The Magazine of Sciences or the True Art of Memory*, discovered by Schenkelius, Paris, 1623
62 a–d Alphabets on the themes of cuisine and wild flowers. Executed in pen and ink by fourteen and fifteen year old children
62 a and b *below* Cuisine

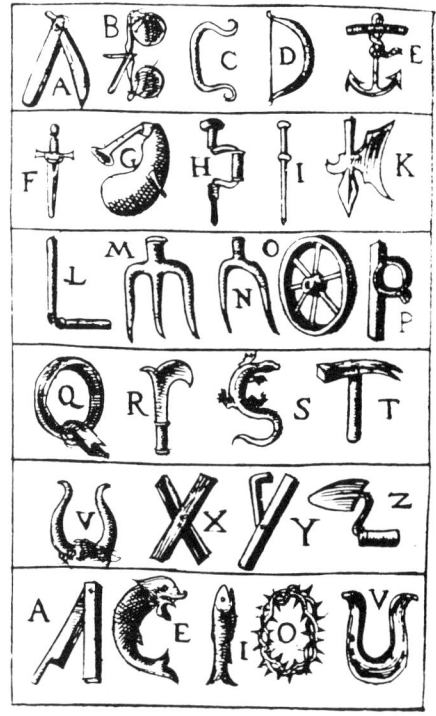

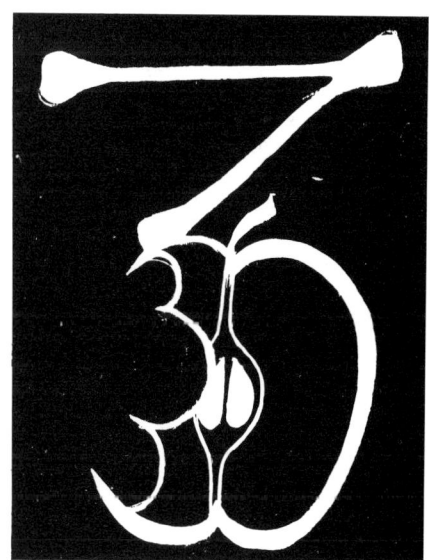

62 c and d   Flowers

A similar project to that in Chapter 5 is the thematic collage. See figure 63. It is a study in basic letter-forms. 70 mm (2¾ in.) sided squares are drawn, four horizontally, four vertically to form a grid. Each of these squares is then formed into a letter by the minimum of chipping away. As soon as it reads as a letter, the chipping stops. This is done both from the outside edge and the inside counter-spaces. After all twelve rectangles have been treated in this manner, some link-up is established between two or three neighbouring letters by shading with dark and mid-tones so that new shapes are created.

These are traced down, ignoring the original grid-lines and using only the newly abstracted shapes. Reinforce these so that they provide a clear guide for the subsequent collage. Tracings of the individual shapes can be made as patterns for fabric pieces.

63   *below and overleaf*   Thematic collage by a fourteen year old girl
a   Shaded drawing of chipped-away rectangles

If no obvious letter-forms remain at the conclusion of this exercise it is of no consequence. The important and relevant part of this project is the chipping. The theme, as before, can be simple or subtle according to the individual's choice.

This scheme need not employ the enlarging process necessary in the name unit collage.

63b *above* Areas marked out
63c *below* Completed collage made of nets, photographs, wallpapers, thread and raffia, in silver, grey, cream, white and black

7 print and printing

Print

Using ready printed areas is no new medium for picture-making. Teachers have long since recognised its usefulness in interpreting tonal contrasts. When designs are being planned and density or tones need sorting out, equivalents in black and white and 'greys' can be made by pasting down printed areas. Conversely, to teach tonal values of colour, children can try to follow a painting, preferably starting with one that has a *range* of colours rather than many different ones, and interpret it in black and white print. Alternatively, the children can first make a 'grey' picture, and then do several versions of it, each in one colour only, taking this colour right through from full strength to white. A simple picture of the children's own making is preferable to a grid, which can be rather dull. A selection of flower or animal shapes, or perhaps buildings, will make the process more enjoyable, and also be better for classroom display.

The use of the printed page is extremely helpful in teaching the value of straightforward black and white. It can be followed by work in pen and ink. Rich results can also be achieved in pictorial collages using this medium of print and paste. The 'literary landscapes' and portraits (figures 64 and 65) show that the restrictions of this technique do not hamper the child.

The landscapes were made to fill the paper completely and the planning of the composition was given much importance. The aim was to try to achieve a sense of scale and a feeling of distance, therefore the actual selection of printed matter was given consideration. Too great a tonal contrast meant that some areas 'stood out' too much. Sometimes there was confusion between one shape and another, requiring a change of tone. Working too closely to the picture is the commonest mistake, and frequent standing back to see the total effect is necessary. It is a good idea to start with the formula of far distance, middle distance, and close-up. Allow an occasional use of photographic matter in addition to the printed areas, but it should be emphasised that one wants to achieve, for example, the effect of water not by sticking down a whole water picture, but by carefully choosing small pieces of black and white, making the *text* undulate. Rushes and tendrils can be stuck down partially and curled; this can relieve the flat surface of the picture and give it added interest.

64 Literary landscapes by thirteen and fourteen year old children
a *right* Pine forest
b *opposite* Skyscraper: view from the street

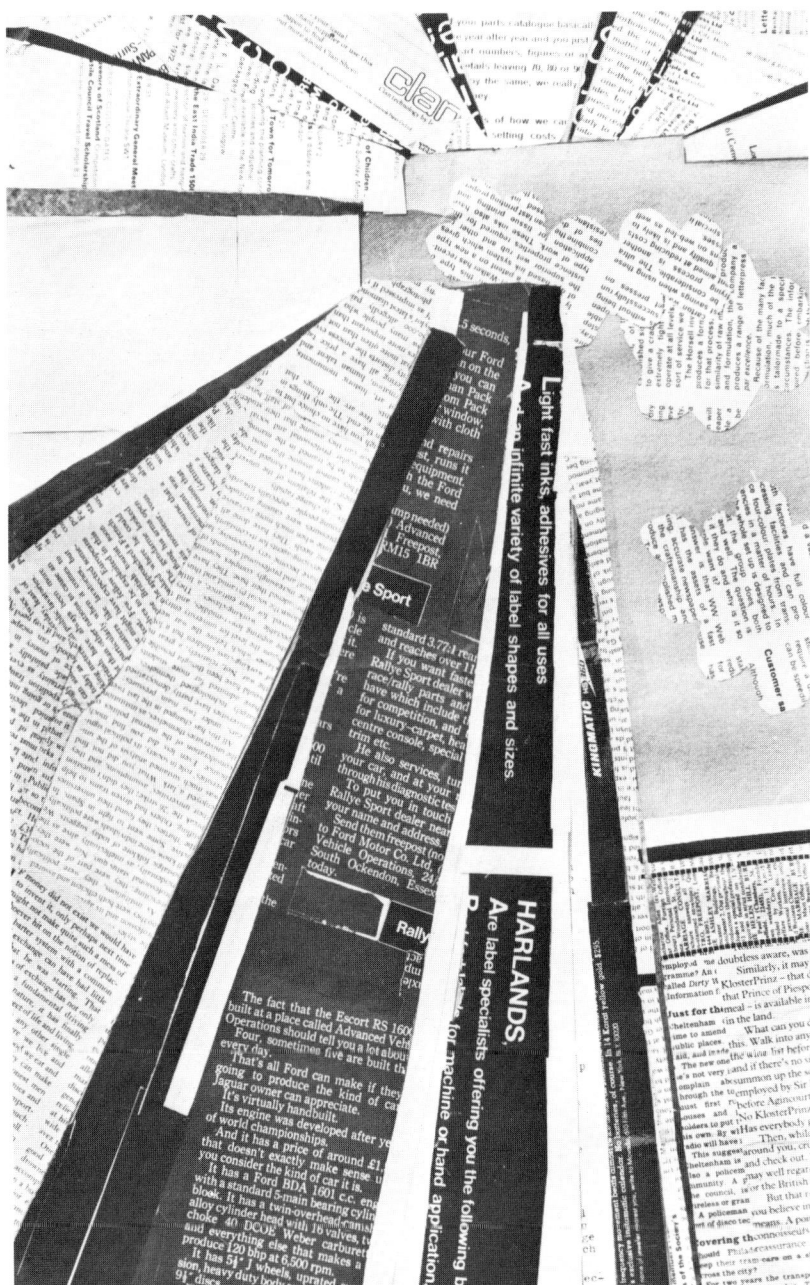

59

The portraits were either imaginary or taken from actual photographs. The background was not considered in this instance and all the concentration was on the face itself, its expression, and the character of the hair.

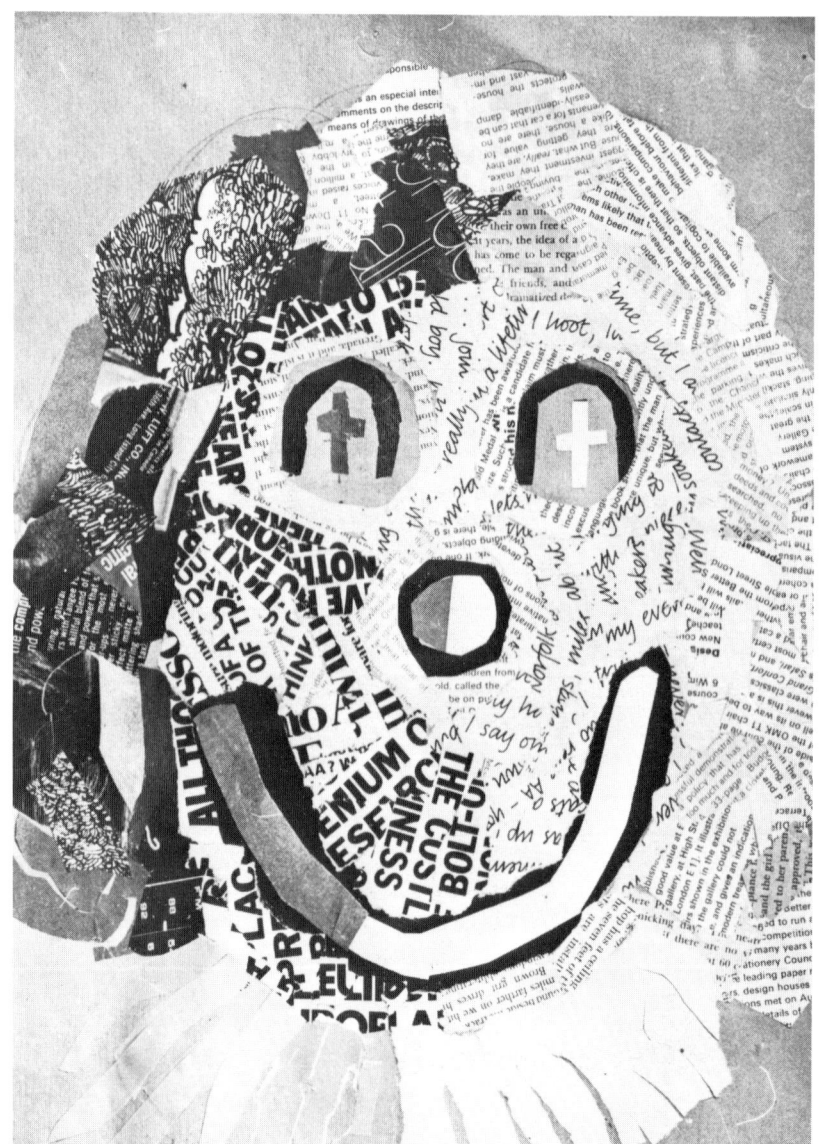

65   Portraits by twelve year old children

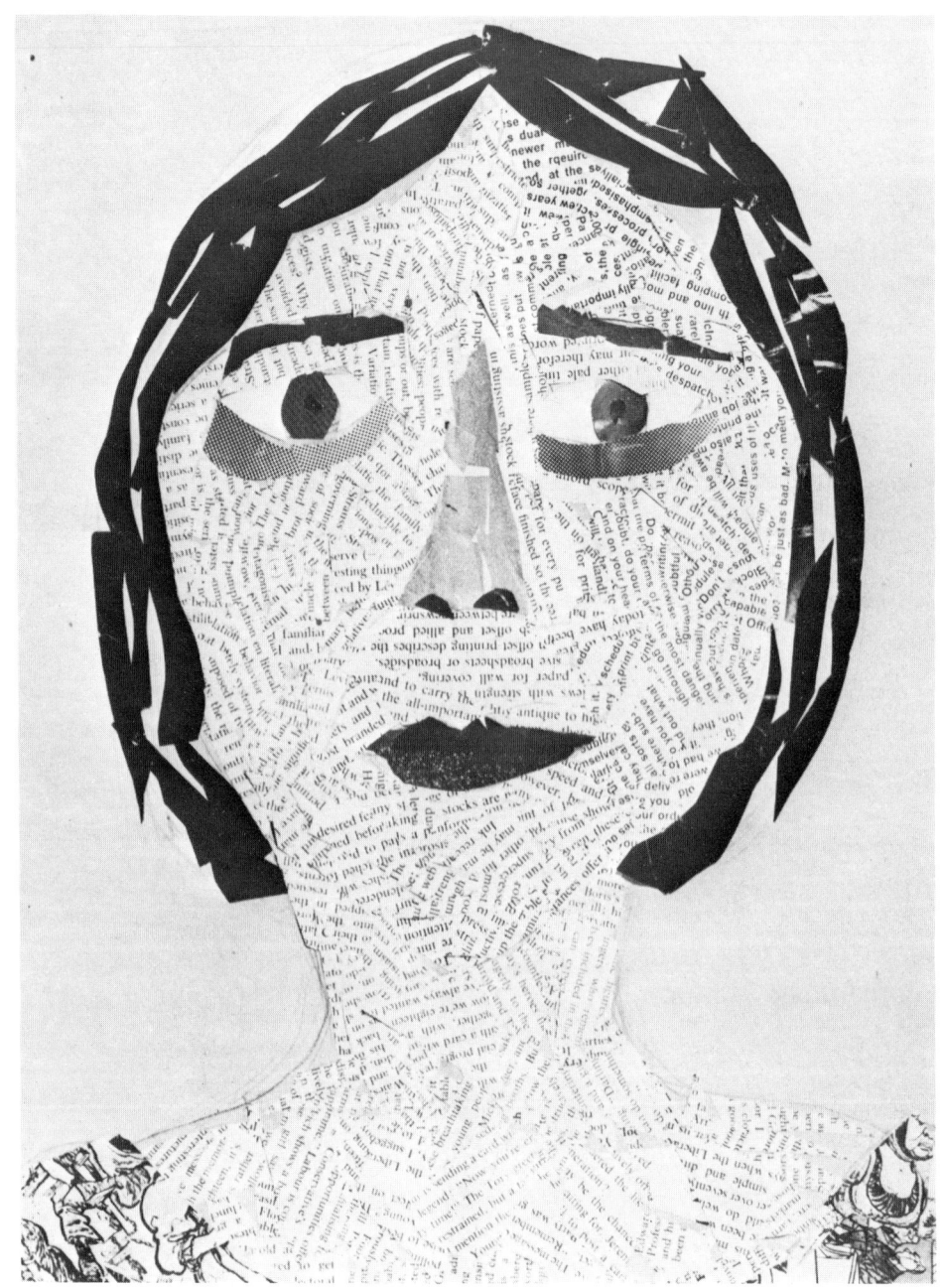

65c   Portrait by a twelve
year old child

Another version of this scheme is to take a theme such as 'hair' and to make an assemblage using letter-forms and photographs. See figure 66. This is an introduction to a poster-style approach and encourages careful selection and arrangement, and the use of random and meaningful letter combinations.

66 Montage with the theme of hair by a fourteen year old girl

Printing

If there are resources for the setting of type or using actual wooden or metal letters, there will be further opportunities for free experiment with letters as well as for teaching the disciplines of the craft of printing. The value of picture-making with letters is that it can allow the child, inhibited perhaps with drawing technique, to 'draw' with the letter, by printing it repeatedly. The fact that he has created a picture in this manner will give him confidence to go on further.

The examples shown in figure 67 have employed very simple methods and could be adapted to the classroom without specialist equipment. The two illustrations have been built up by the repetition of one or two letters, either wood or metal. Balsa wood, card or lino could be substituted if a handle is put on for ease of printing.

67　Printed pictures by thirteen year old boys
a　Cat
b　Cup of tea

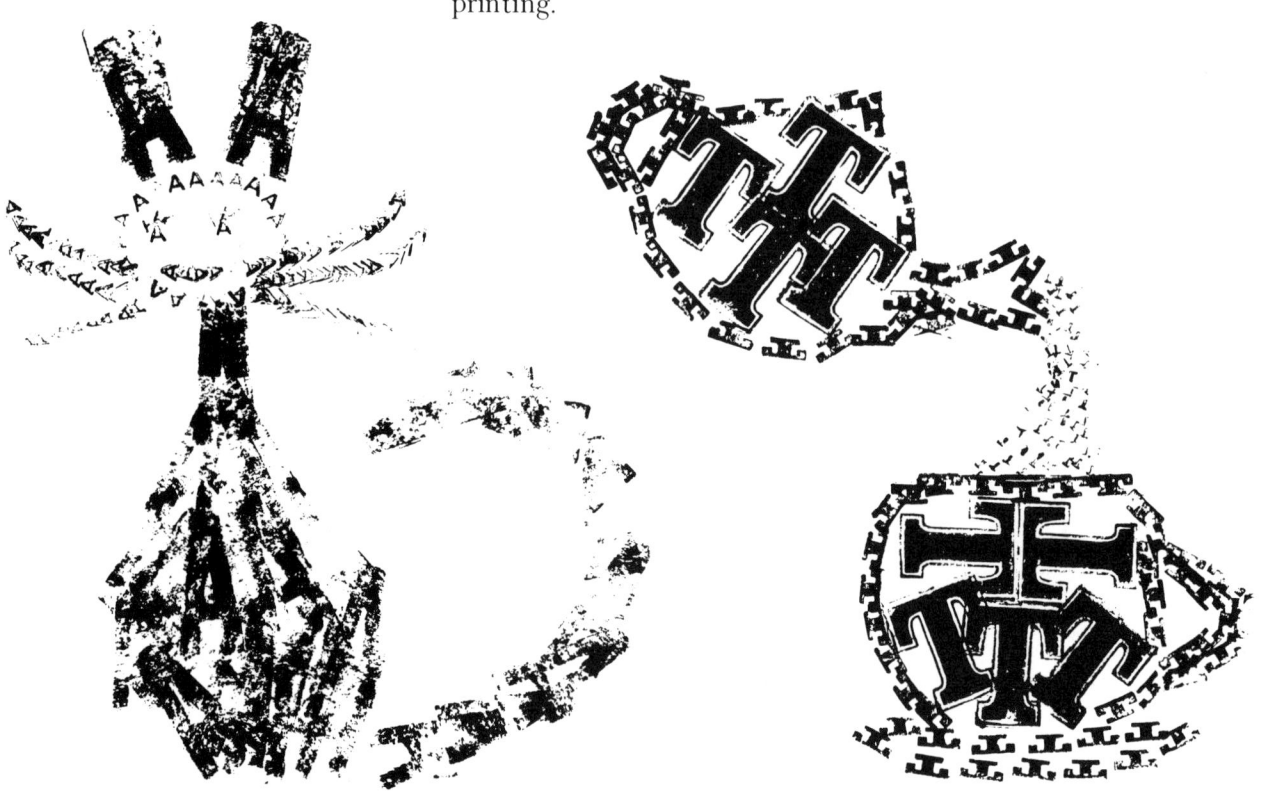

The circular 'plate' in oranges and blacks, uses wooden letters in a decorative manner, creating interesting shapes and patterns (figure 68).

68 Motif made from the repetition of A, T and Y wooden letters by a student

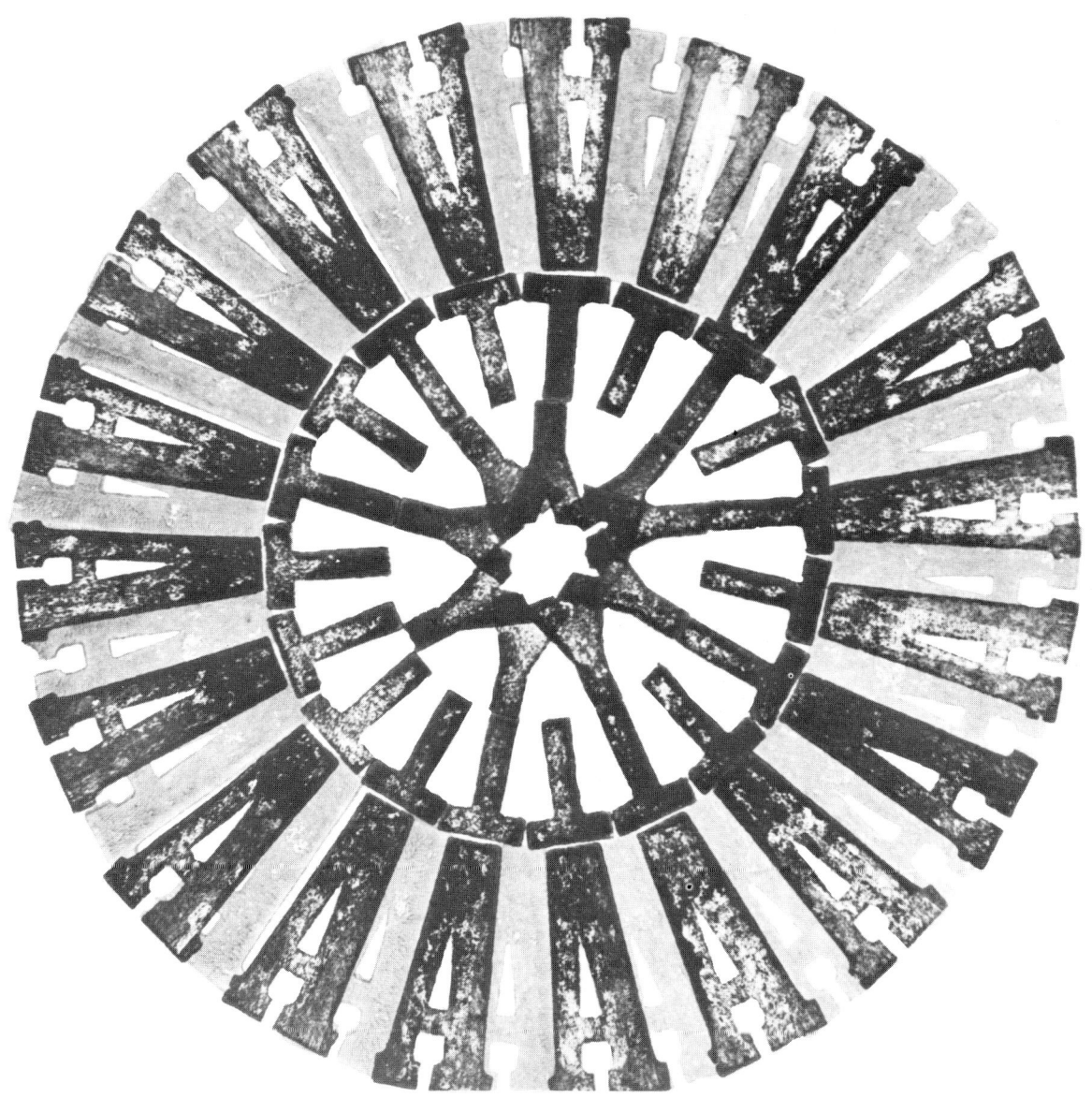

69 Poster printed with a wooden typeface in shades of black ink by fourteen year old boys

Drugs kill. In this school poster produced and printed by fourteen year old boys (figure 69), there is good use of space and repetition to create the effect of being gradually overcome and diminished with a final, positive destruction. It has far more impact than if the two words had been printed singly. The falling off of the last 'L' emphasises the power of the drugs to over-balance, perhaps fatally. This is a 'working word' in the context of poster design (*Working Words*, page 86).

The boxes shown in figure 76 have been made up in cartridge paper and rolled up with flat colour. The letters have been placed in such a way as to decorate the surfaces, and to make the box interesting from every viewpoint. The 'E's are arranged in one instance to form an 'H'.

70 Cartridge paper boxes made by sixteen year old boys. The boxes have been decorated with two letterforms, or one placed to create another (E to H). Black ink on paper rolled up in bright pink

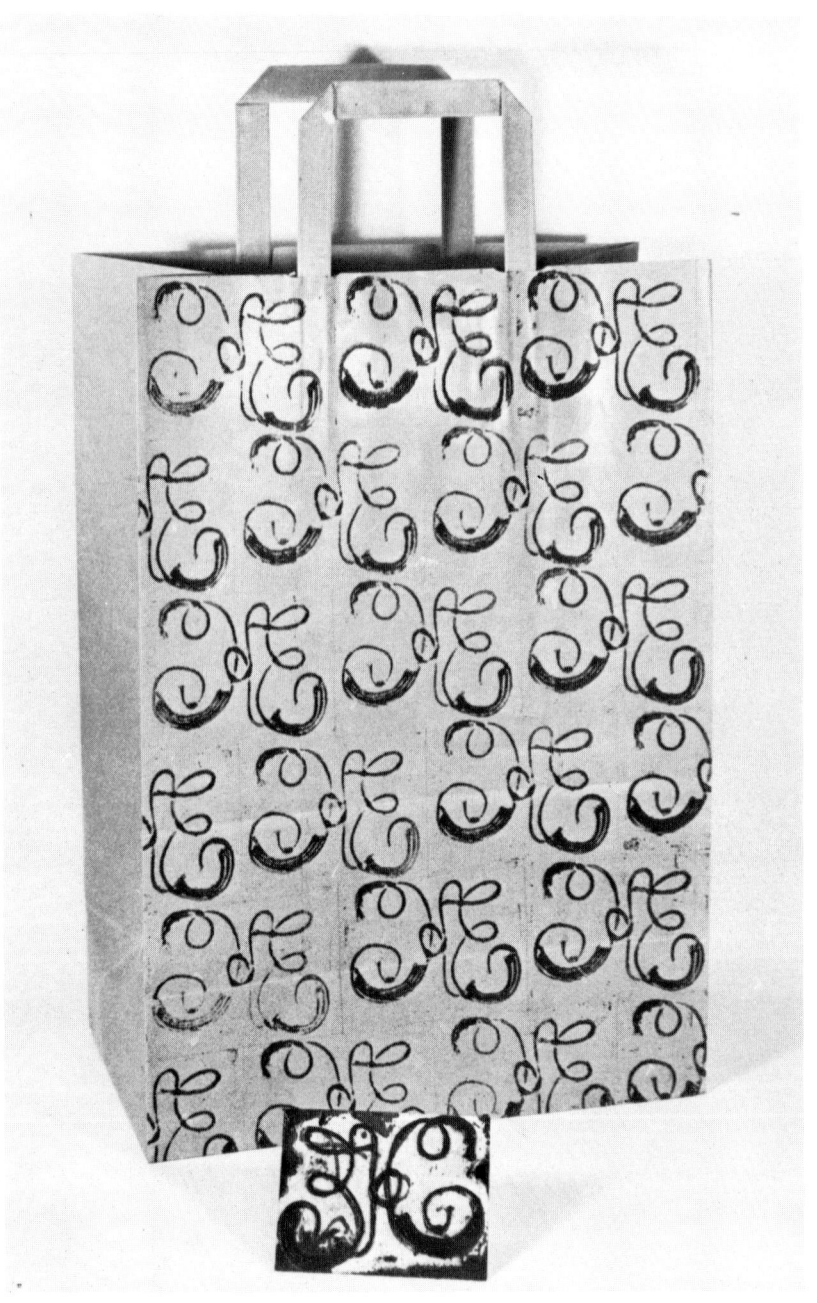

71　KE.　Scrolled initials made with
string glued on to a card backing.
Printed in water-based ink, dark blue on
a pink paper carrier bag, by a fifteen year
old girl

A carrier-bag is decorated with a flourished 'KE', printed in dark blue on a pink paper bag (figure 71). The block is shown made from string glued on to cardboard with PVA adhesive. This was printed with water-based ink.

In this gouache painting the central letter is a Letraset 'G' (figure 72). This exercise in tonal values uses the rhythms of the capital letter which are echoed in layers of restricted colour, in this instance primary red and the addition of black and white only.

72 Gouache painting by a fourteen year old boy

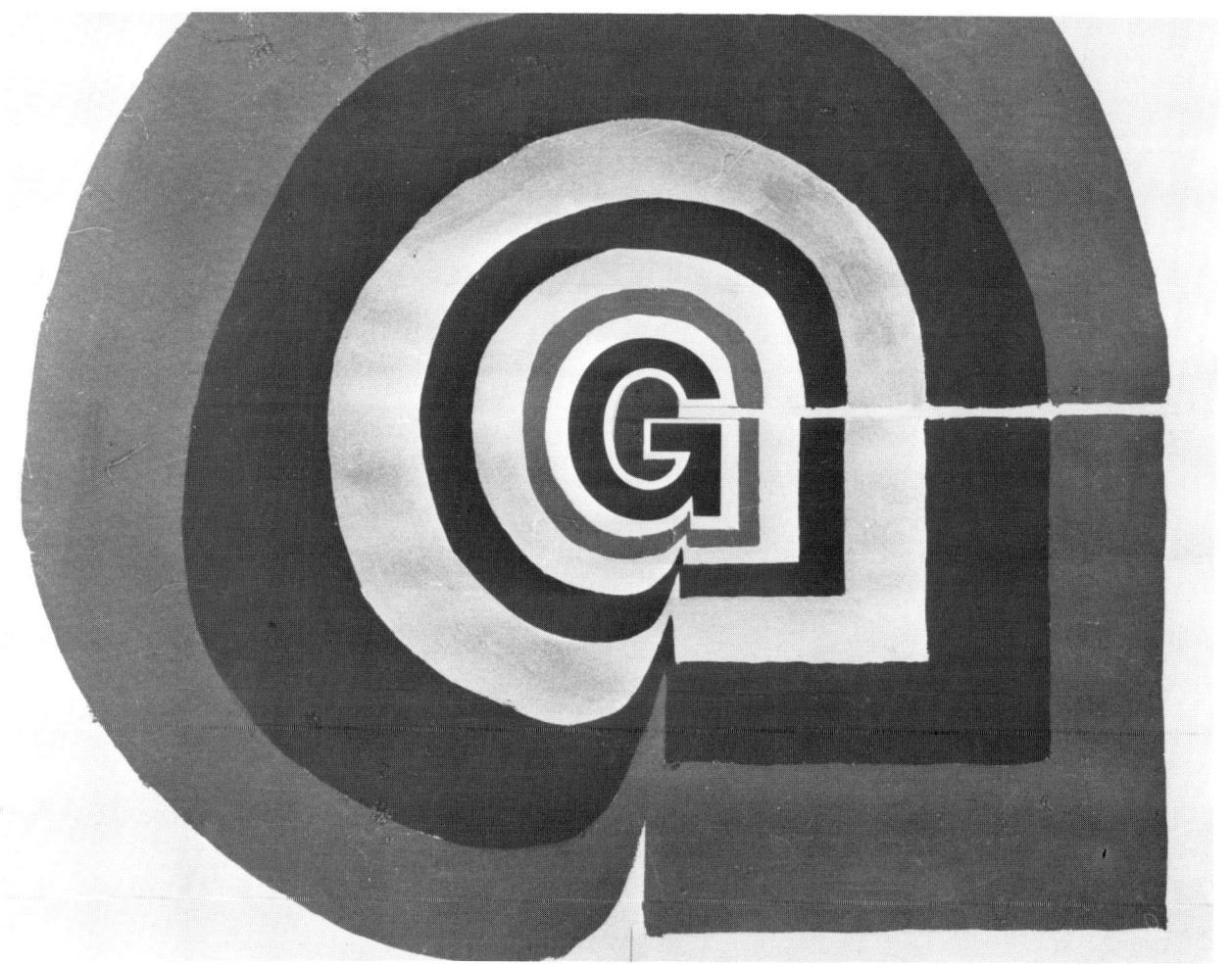

In figure 73 Letraset letters have been used in conjunction with pen and ink drawing to form small decorative design units. These can later be developed into block or screen prints on paper or fabric. Designs drawn directly on to *Kodatrace* can be transferred photographically on to a silk screen.

73   Letraset and pen drawings by Mary Newland

8 patterns and poems

Words or sentences that are not understood and have no meaning to the reader become gestures. Like the runic inscriptions, they can be decorations rather than meaningful combinations of symbols.

The gesture is like a doodle – a product of the unconscious mind. It may contain static constructions, such as dots and geometric figures, or simple, rhythmic linear patterns. It may contain animated forms, reminiscent of the grotesque living patterns found in medieval manuscripts.

The action of doodling shows a reversion to the delights of scribbling in our earlier years. This inherent feeling for pattern-making appears later in the formed handwriting, but this has had

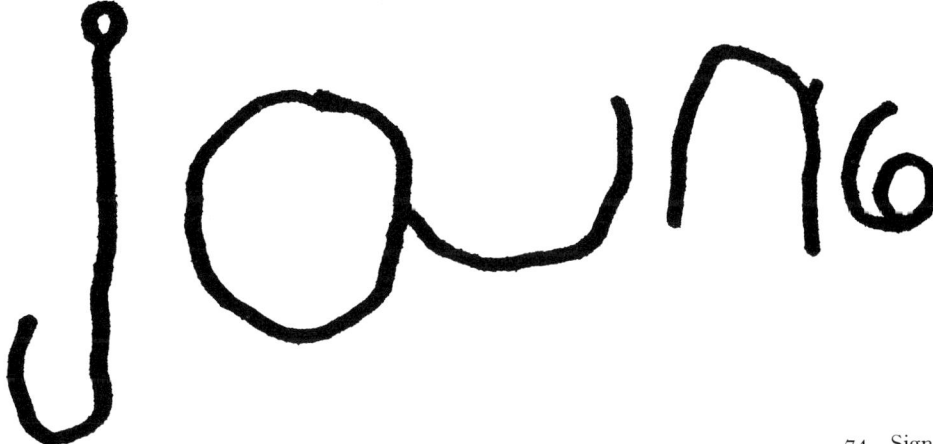

74 Signature by a four year old girl

75 Page from a sixteenth-century Italian manuscript. Reproduced by courtesy of the Victoria and Albert Museum

the spontaneity suppressed in order to render the symbols meaningful.

However, the actual physical act of writing renders every mark unique and graphologists maintain that our writing manifests our personality.

Patterns

Writing *patterns* can help to bring back the flow and rhythm to writing; rhythm and writing are inseparable. Chinese calligraphers are encouraged to let the movement flow right from the shoulder down to the fingertips. Calligraphy has been called action painting par excellence, and although with the Western alphabet it is more difficult to convey this sensuous feeling, nevertheless it is possible for writing to be beautifully made, and made beautiful.

The vocabulary of writing can be extended by the collection and use of all kinds of writing tools: quills, twigs, straws, all types of brushes, crayons and pens. Sample sheets can be made with these implements, using also different inks, and a portion of the rhythmical pattern-making can then be selected and the countershapes and interspaces coloured in. The whole unit can then be enlarged and interpreted in threads, to echo the linear rhythms, and paint or fabric pieces to emphasise the larger shapes. See figure 76. Using a trailer for the glue will help to sustain the flowing rhythms. Slightly diluted resin glue will be quite manageable in a plastic detergent bottle, or better still, a smaller adhesive container which fits the hand more comfortably.

A good loosening-up exercise is to make a mixture of flour and water, taking care to get rid of all the lumps, and to make name or letter patterns on strong paper. It must be left flat until it is completely dry, to avoid running (figure 77). This technique is often used to create raised effects on theatrical costume and is drawn similarly on stretched fabric. When dry it is sprayed with colour. There are possibilities here for blazonry, etc.

The research and work of Marion Richardson provided an outlet for the creative impulse of the child. The practice and invention of new patterns was encouraged in the early 1930s. Simple writing rhythms were established, based on the letters of the alphabet.

76 Writing patterns with follow-up work in crayon and collage by a twelve year old girl

77 Trail writing on sugar paper by a thirteen year old girl, using a flour and water mixture in a detergent bottle

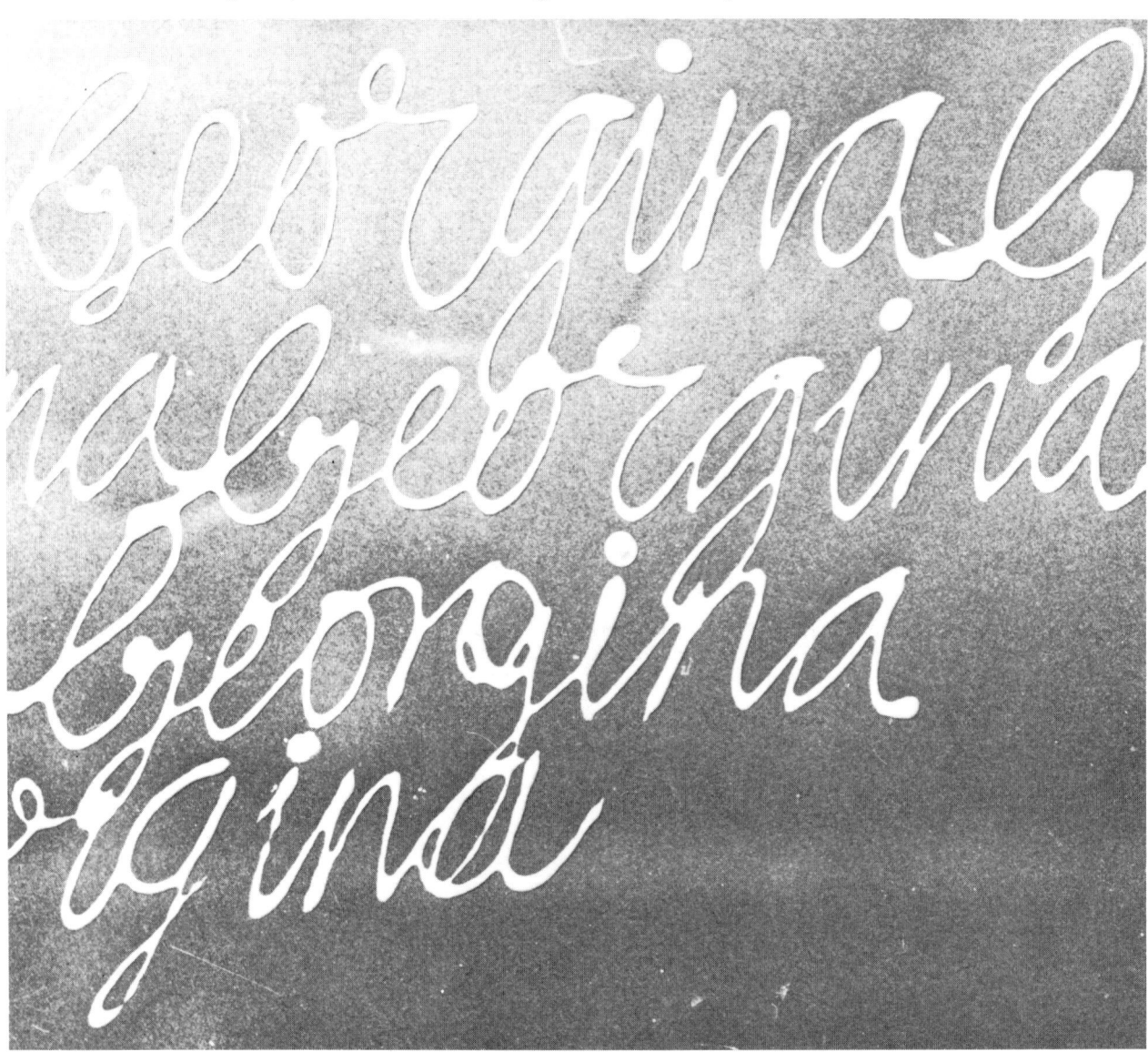

Shaped writing

The physical acts of writing and drawing are inextricably linked. This is perfectly illustrated in the letter from Vincent van Gogh where visual and verbal notes become one, both complementary to each other. Here the artist and the author are autonomous. When an author illustrates his own work, it rarely proves successful. Two, quite separate, skills are involved, and few are gifted with equal brilliance. Some exceptions are William Blake, Edward Lear and James Thurber.

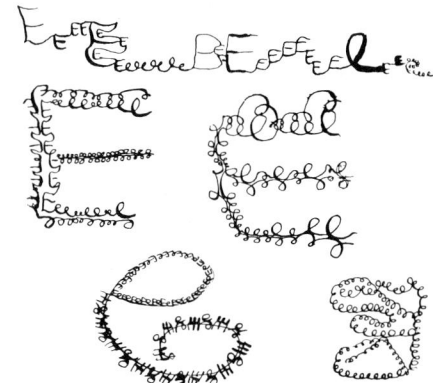

78 Examples of practice with a pen, using one letter as the subject, by a fourteen year old girl

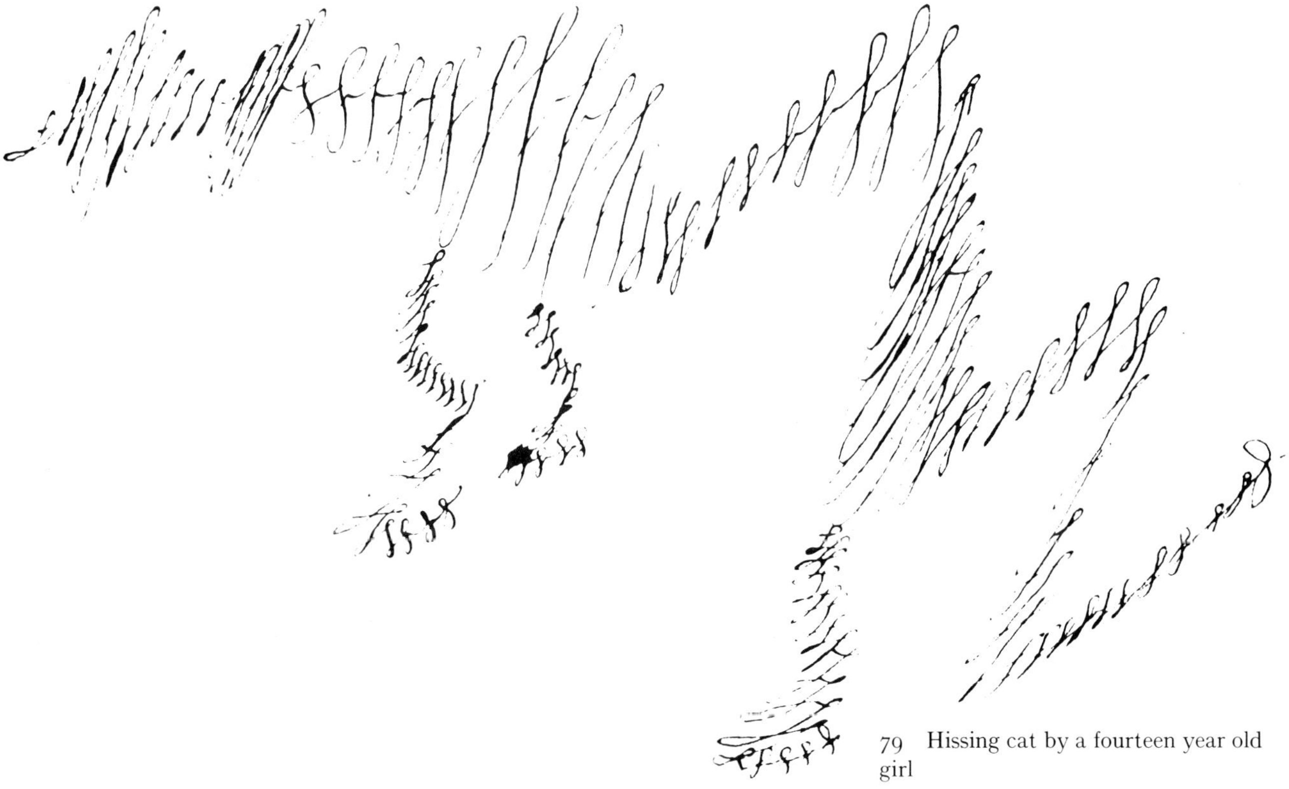

79 Hissing cat by a fourteen year old girl

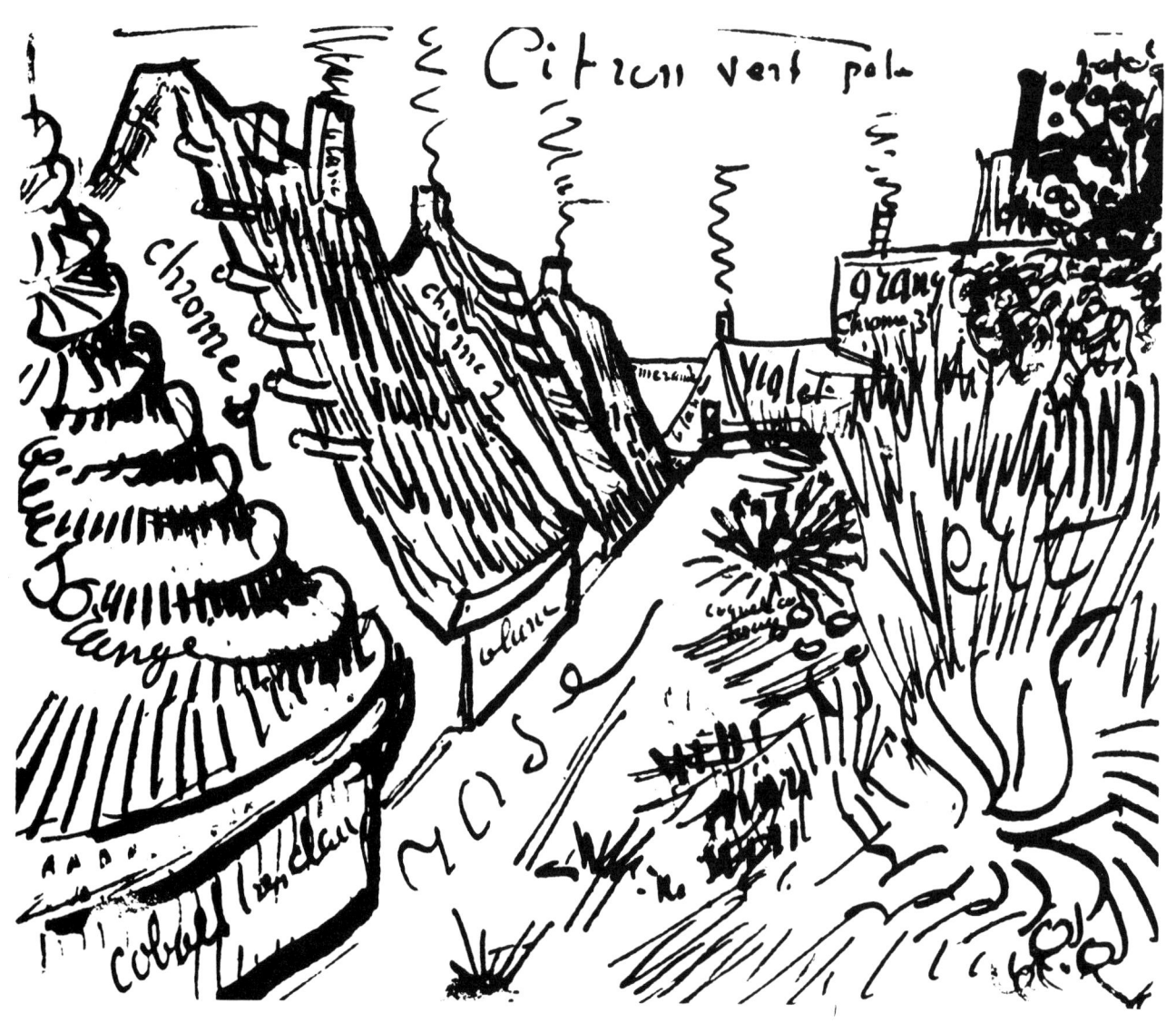

80   Drawing by Vincent Van Gogh,
taken from a letter to Emile Bernard
written at Arles in June 1888. National
Museum Vincent Van Gogh, Amsterdam

A

a

A was once an apple-pie,
  Pidy
  Widy
  Tidy
  Pidy
Nice insidy
Apple-Pie.

B

b

B was once a little bear,
  Beary!
  Wary!
  Hairy!
  Beary!
Taky cary!
Little Bear!

C

c

C was once a little cake,
  Caky,
  Baky
  Maky
  Caky,
Taky Caky,
Little Cake!

D

d

D was once a little doll,
  Dolly,
  Molly,
  Polly
  Nolly,
Nursy Dolly,
Little Doll!

81 Part of one of Edward Lear's
alphabets

P was a pig
That was not very big
But his tail was too
Curly
And that made him surly
P! cross little Pig!

82   Painted versions of the Lear
alphabet poems, with additional thread
and sequins, by eleven year old girls
a   *above* Pig
b   *opposite* Cat

Writing that forms an actual picture falls into a different category of its own. *Calligrams* are a combination of written or printed text, thought and design. They can be designed to be read, or be virtually indecipherable. They attempt to fuse poetic thought with visual language. The Latin alphabet is not so easily adapted to this form as the graceful half-uncials, and more manipulative still are the Arabic scripts. In the Far East the art of calligraphy has always merged with the arts of painting and poetry.

Incredible photographic writing-portraits have been popular (including a notable one of Queen Victoria, consisting of 173,000 words relating an historical account of her reign!) Advertisers have used this method of picture-building with words with good effect more recently.

83 A Latin calligram showing Cygnus (the Swan). This is part of the poem *Phaenomena* by Aratus of Soli of the third century BC, translated by Cicero, and made into a calligram by a scribe in the ninth or tenth century AD. Reproduced by courtesy of the British Museum

84 A nineteenth-century portrait of Ono-no-Komachi, one of the famous six poets of ancient Japan, by Hokusai. The thirty-one syllable poem reads 'A flower with no outward sign is the heart of a man in this world.' The robes of the poet are a calligraphic representation of her name. Reproduced by courtesy of the British Museum

85 Examples of shaped writing
a *below left* *The Waterfall* by a nine year old child
b *right* *The Church* by a twelve year old child

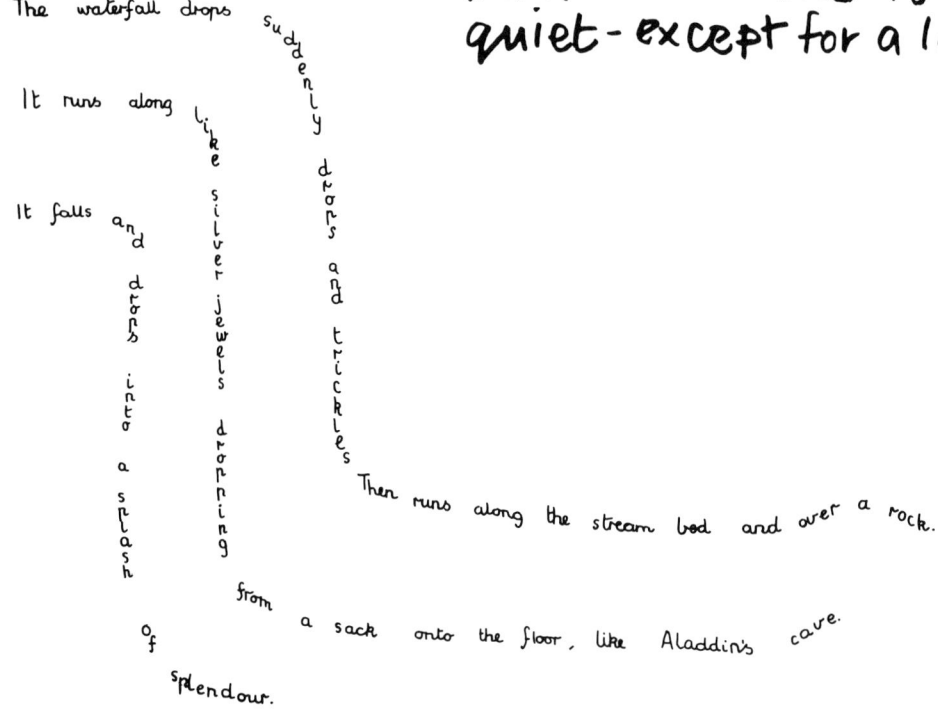

t
he
Church
Stood on the hill
Old as the sea and weather beaten
Protec ting a tree, guarding a forest of tombsto ne heads—looking o ut over the rose-beds
the ch urch st ood, dingy and
Dark with no-one to disturb the
quiet - except for a lark-singing-

The waterfall drops suddenly

It runs along like silver jewels dropping

It falls and drops into a splash of

drops and trickles

Then runs along the stream bed and over a rock.

from a sack onto the floor, like Aladdin's cave.

Splendour.

Poems

Shaped poems can be set in type or written by hand. The latter is more flexible and renders the picture-poem idea available to anyone with pencil and paper to hand.

Hella Basu's work shows a real delight in letterforms. See figure 88. She manipulates these to create expressive illustrations to the poetry and prose of others. Much of her work has developed from devising visual aids as a lecturer in graphic design, where she is demonstrating the use of letterforms for different purposes, their ability to enhance a given meaning, historical associations or psychological feelings. Her work attempts to bring letters to life, using them to form textures and patterns relating to a given verbal message, so combining intellectual and visual experience.

86   *The Beast* by a fifteen year old girl

87 *right* *Our Lady's Shoes were Glacé Kid*. From the Folder *To Catch a Whiteman by his Manifestoe* by Dom Sylvester Houédard, designed by Stephen Lowndes. Reproduced by courtesy of the Victoria and Albert Museum

88 *opposite* A silk screen print by Hella Basu, showing the first verse of John Donne's poem *Hymn to God, my God in my sickness*

what tiny
shiny concealing
exciting adorable
shoes congealed that
tip toe touch of such a
lovely foot on top my cresc-
ent moon light heart spiked
its pleasuring heel to grind
my mind to snaky bliss or
supported its swan necked
arch to shop along the
endless streets of my
down town soul &
tread my lava
layered lime-
stone hills that

what tiny
shiny concealing
exciting adorable
shoes congealed that
tip toe touch of such a
lovely foot on top my cresc-
ent moon light heart spiked
its pleasuring heel to grind
my mind to snaky bliss or
supported its swan necked
arch to shop along the
endless streets of my
down town soul &
tread my lava
layered lime-
stone hills that

our ladies shoes were glace kid

or country brogues

are always
making me
remind her
of galilee

are always
making me
remind her
of galilee

84

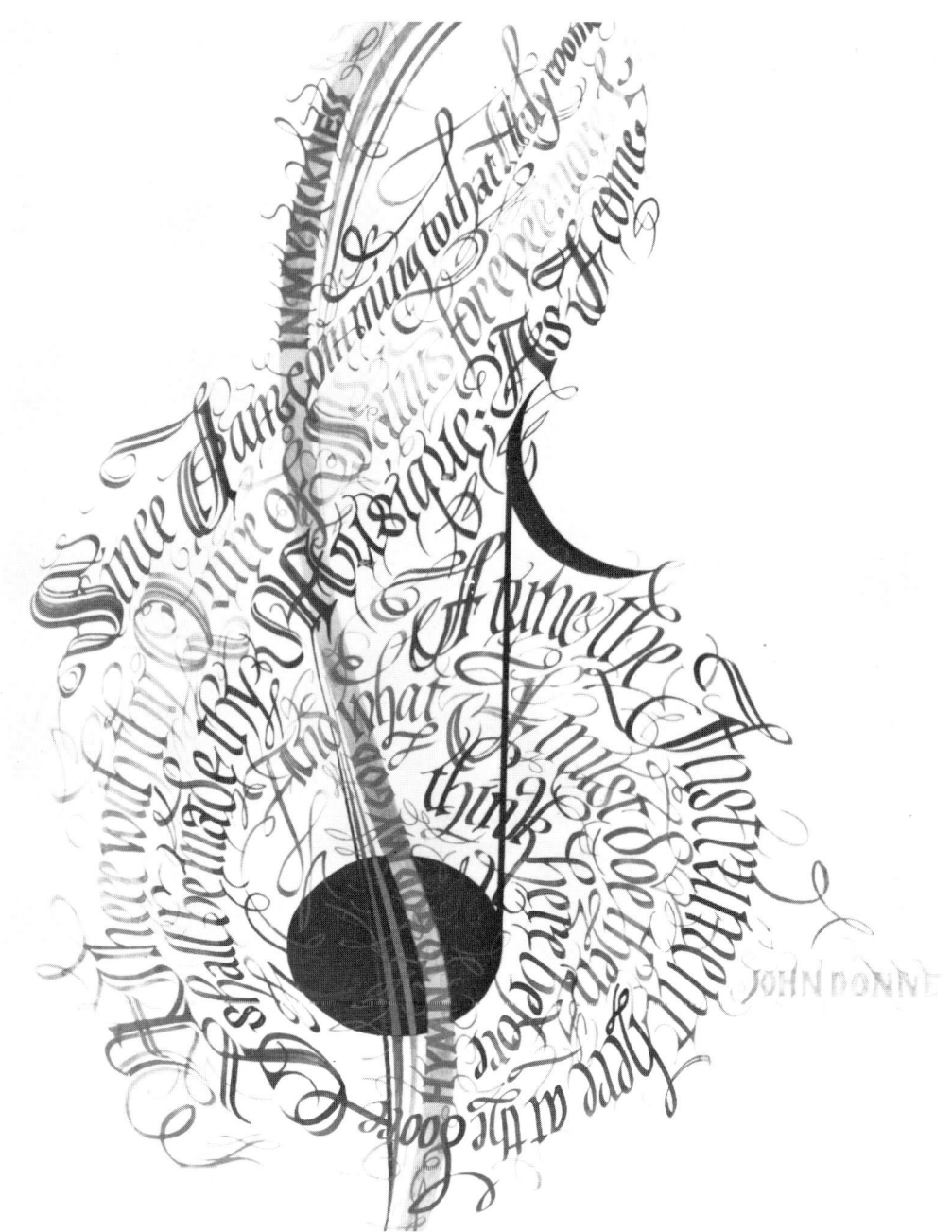

9 working words

Making an actual symbol from the letters which form its name is an exercise for the intellect.

It is a device in constant use in advertising media as it has the obvious merit of saying the same thing *twice*, in verbal and in visual terms. Whereas the shaped poem or calligram often lost its literary meaning by being re-arranged from the conventional left-to-right reading order, this way of using letters demands legibility, give or take a certain amount of distortion.

89 War and Peace. Painted poster with additional crayon by a fourteen year old girl

A 'working words' scheme can be presented in two parts, both suitable for the older school child or student.

First, select an object, simple in shape, and draw it very lightly in outline so that this serves as a guide only, *not* as a statement. Arrange the descriptive letters of the object within the line. Distortion will inevitably arise, therefore care must be taken to find the best solution without losing the legibility of the letters and consequently, the word. The result should be well balanced, and self criticism, rather than an easy way out of the problem, should be encouraged.

These criteria also apply to the second version. Here the approach is a more expressive one. The word should describe a mood or situation, in other words, an abstract conception. Clever or crude examples of this can be found in advertising media, comics and magazines.

90 *below and following* Designs by fourteen and fifteen year old children carried out in cut, coloured papers
a Bite

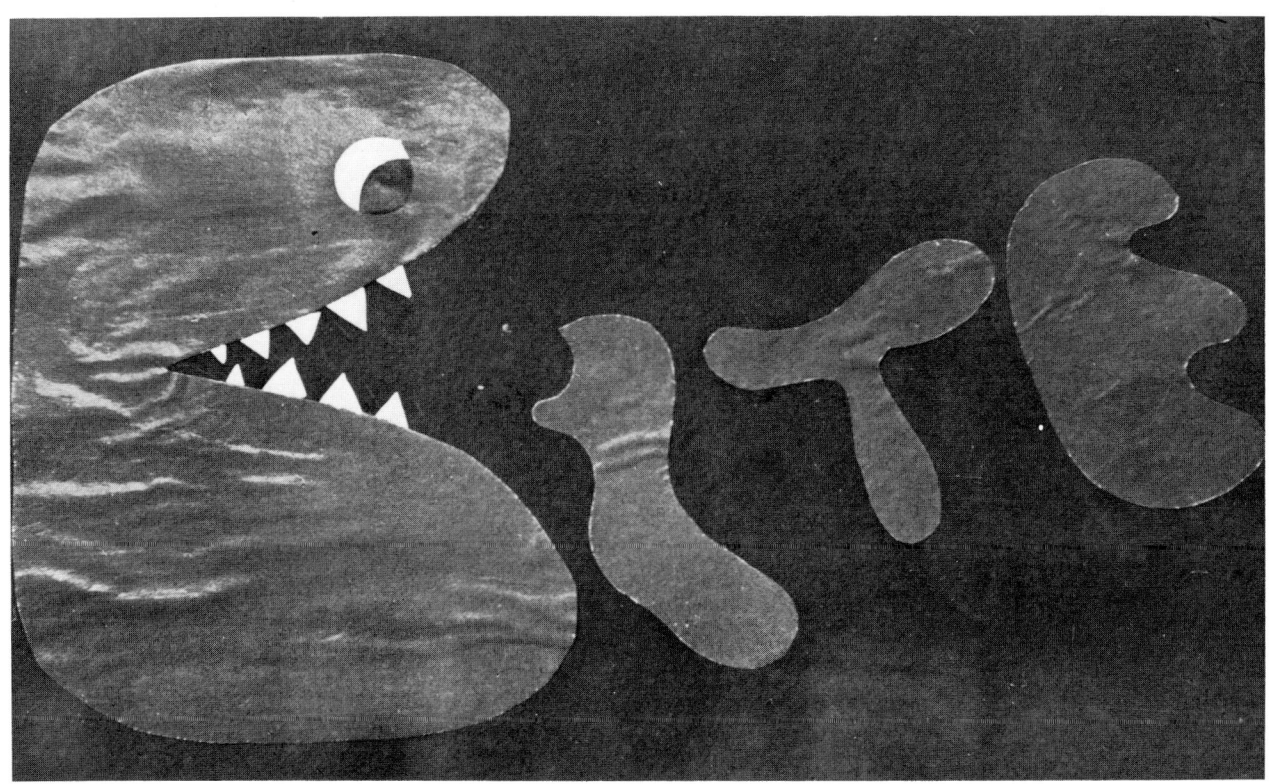

If a situation or action of an extreme nature is being expressed, such as 'stretch', it is important to remember that it is not each *individual* letter that tells the tale but the word as a whole.

There is plenty of scope using these two approaches with quite simple ideas. They can be subtle or basic according to the individual's capabilities, but they should always be the child's or student's own ideas. Story-boards (the panels used by television designers to show each frame of a moving picture), could be devised, and discussion, the critical appraisal of professional work in this medium, should be encouraged.

90b Kettle
90c *opposite* Hide

90d　Ice cream (the dot of the I is a
little red cherry)

90e   Shadow

90f   Beckon

conclusion

'Good instruction in letter design is . . . a specific art-training medium of great value' (Von Larisch, *Unterricht in Ornamentaler Schrift*, Staatsdruckerei).

Von Larisch devised a teaching programme for his students to develop their creative abilities. He tried to help them to understand the rhythm and harmonious unity that good designing should have. He encouraged them to use all kinds of tools so that they would have a well-rounded approach to the use and creation of letterforms.

It seems a very long distance to travel from scratched messages on clay, drying in the sun to '. . . a fifteen second "link" (TV), all washed down the electronic plughole with the rest of the flow'. Nevertheless both the tablet and the box are forms of communication using the letter as their agent.

Von Larisch, in the first part of this century, taught good lettering through the means of an art-based curriculum. It would seem equally desirable to reverse the procedure, and teach some of the aspects of good art education through the medium of the letter.

91 *Graphics*. Panel by Marlene Pickard.
Collage made of padded suède and
leather with stainless steel rod, size
100 cm × 46 cm (39½ in × 18 in.).
Collection of Leicestershire County
Council

bibliography

The Miraculous Birth of Language, Richard Albert Wilson, Dent, London

From Cave Painting to Comic Strip, Lancelot Hogben, Max Parrish, London

The History and Technique of Lettering, Alexander Nesbitt, Dover, New York

Lascaux, Annette Laming, Penguin, Harmondsworth

A Book of Scripts, Alfred Fairbank, Penguin, Harmondsworth

Fun with Pens, Christopher Jarman, Black, London

The word as Image, Berjouhi Bowler, Studio Vista, London

The Complete Nonsense of Edward Lear, Edited by Holbrook Jackson, Faber, London

The Passport, Saul Steinberg, Hamish Hamilton, London

There's Motion Everywhere, John Travers Moore, Nelson, London

Counterblast, Marshall McLuhan, Rapp and Whiting, London

Letter and Image, Massin, Studio Vista, London

Lettering as Drawing, Nicolette Gray, Oxford University Press, London and New York

Signs, Symbols and Signets, Ernst Lehner, Dover, New York

Trademarks and Symbols of the World, Yusaku Kamekura, Studio Vista, London

Lettera 1 and Lettera 2, Haab/haettenschweiler, Arthur Nigli, Zurich

The Book of Signs, Rudolph Koch, Dover, New York

The Complete Works of Lewis Carroll, The Nonesuch Press, London

Design as Art, Bruno Munari, Penguin, Harmondsworth

The Development of Writing, Carol Donoghue, Jackdaw Publications No. 47, Cape, London

Lettering for Embroidery, Pat Russell, Batsford, London; Van Nosward Reinhold, New York

Lettering Today, John Brinkley, Studio Vista, London

Pictorial Alphabets, Ruari McLean, Studio Vista, London

TV Graphics, Roy Laughton, Studio Vista, London

The Gutenberg Galaxy, Marshall McLuhan, University of Toronto Press

Sign, Image and Symbol, Edited by Gyorgy Kepes, Studio Vista, London

Illiteracy; a world problem, Sir Charles Jeffries, Pall Mall Press, London

Signs of the Zodiac, Victoria and Albert Museum, HMSO, London

Unterricht in Ornamentaler Schrift, Rudolf von Larisch, Staatsdruckerei, Vienna

The author and publisher would like to thank the following for their kind permission to reproduce illustrations included in the book:

Dover Publications, Inc for figures 4, 7, 18, 20, 21, 22, 23, 24, and 28 from *Signs, Symbols and Signets* by Ernst Lehner, 1969; figure 19 from *The Book of Signs* by Rudolf Koch.

Faber and Faber Limited for figure 9 from *Background to Chinese Art* by H G Porteus, 1935.

The Leicestershire County Council for figure 91, and the Embroiderers' Guild for supplying the photograph.

The Openings Press from Bath Academy for figure 87 from *To Catch a Whiteman by his Manifestoe* by Dom Sylvester Houédard, designed by Stephen Lowndes.

The Radio Times Hulton Picture Library for figure 5.